NOTES FOR THE

STUDY & EXPOSITION

OF 1ST JOHN

NOTES FOR THE STUDY & EXPOSITION OF 1ST JOHN

ERIC E. KRESS

Kress Christian
PUBLICATIONS

Published by:
Kress Christian Publications
P.O. Box 132228
The Woodlands, TX 77393

Scripture taken from the NEW AMERICAN STANDARD BIBLE®
© Copyright The Lockman Foundation 1960, 1962, 1963, 1968, 1971, 1972, 1973, 1975, 1977
Used by permission. (www.Lockman.org)

ISBN 0-9717568-0-5

Cover Design & Book Layout: D.M. Battermann, R&D Design Services

Acknowledgments

• • • • • •

The author would like to thankfully acknowledge Dr. Irv Busenitz of The Master's Seminary, Dr. Bill Smallman of Baptist Mid-Missions, Dr. Gareth Cockerill of Wesley Biblical Seminary, Garry Knussman of Grace To You, as well as John Lewis and Chet Boyd of O.M. Literature for their encouragement and editorial suggestions.

Contents

● ● ● ● ● ●

Chapter 1
Introduction to 1 John

1. The Writer

The human author is not specifically named within the epistle itself.

A. The Internal Evidence.

1)He was an eyewitness of Christ and the events of the gospel (1:1-3).

2) He had definite, recognized authority among his readers (2:1, 7, 8, 15; 3:7, 18; 4:1-6).

3) He employed a very similar grammar, style and vocabulary as the author of the Gospel of John (cf. 1 John 1:4 and John 16:24; 1 John 4:6 and John 8:47; 1 John 5:12 and John 3:36).

B. The External Evidence

The overwhelming testimony of the early Church points to the Apostle John as the human author of the three epistles known as First, Second and Third John.

The Human Author (John the Apostle)—

Association with Jesus and the transforming work of the Holy Spirit (John 14:16,17; 16:13) had turned an unforgiving (Luke 9:49-56), ambitious, self-seeking (Mark 10:35-45), and sometimes hostile man, once named with James a "Son of Thunder" (Mark 3:17), into the Apostle of love (note the emphasis of love in John 13; 1 John 2:7-11; 3:10-24; 4:7-12; 2 John; 3 John).

The Divine Author—

The Holy Spirit inspired the text of 1 John (cf. 1 Thes. 2:13; 2 Tim. 3:16-17; 2 Pet. 1:20-21;). It thus has absolute authority over our entire lives.

2. The Readers

A. The Original Readers

Unlike the Apostle Paul's epistles, which were addressed to specific people or churches, 1 John's addressees are not mentioned by name. We can see from chapter 2 verses 1 and 12-14 among other places that John was writing to a *community of professing believers at all different maturity levels* who were under his spiritual care. There are no direct quotations, and only one brief mention of the Old Testament (3:12) in the entire epistle (cf. also Prov. 4:18-19 with 1 John 2:10-11). This could indicate a mostly non-Jewish audience.

B. The Current Readers

We must not forget that we too, in God's sovereignty, are the readers. The general nature of the epistle helps us see its immediate application to us.

3. The Reasons

A. To Bring Fellowship

what we *the Apostles* **have seen and heard we proclaim to you also, so that you too may have fellowship with us** *through the apostolic witness*; **and indeed our fellowship is with the Father, and with His Son Jesus Christ** (1 John 1:3).

B. To Complete Joy

These things we write, so that our joy may be made complete (1 John 1:4). There is joy in the sharing and receiving of the truth of Christ.

C. To Grow in Holiness

My little children, I am writing these things to you so that you may not sin (1 John 2:1).

D. To Give Encouragement

I am writing to you, little children, because your sins have been forgiven you for His name's sake. I am writing to you, fathers, because you know Him who has been from the beginning. I am writing to you, young men, because you have overcome the evil one. I have written to you, children, because you know the Father ...(1 John 2:12-14; cf. 2:1-2; 3:1-3; 4:4; 5:13). In light of John's startling descriptions of genuine Christianity (cf. 1 John 2:3-6; 3:4-10; 5:18), he balances the perfect standard of the truth with pastoral encouragement as to God's provision, grace and love.

E. To Fight False Teaching

These things I have written to you concerning those who are trying to deceive you (1 John 2:26; cf. 2:22-23; 4:2). False teachers had infiltrated the Church and were distorting the truth about the Person of Christ, the nature of salvation and even sanctification. First John is a polemic against these distortions. John uses black-and-white terminology to fight the teachers of error. In doing so, he makes statements that at times seem shocking, but as noted above, he is sure to encourage the true believer of God's love and grace.

F. To Promote the Assurance of Eternal Life

These things I have written to you who believe in the name of the Son of God, so that you may know that you have eternal life (1 John 5:13). The content of the entire epistle points to this as being the over-arching theme of the book. Throughout the letter, John gives a series of "snapshots" of genuine Christianity, by which we are to test the validity of our profession of faith and thus **know we have eternal life.** They are not prerequisites for salvation, but evidences of salvation. The only prerequisite for eternal life is faith in Jesus Christ, the Son of God.

4. The Rest of 1 John

Since true Christians have fellowship with God (1 John 1:3), they manifest the character of God and His Son Jesus Christ. First John says:

   a. God is light (1:5)

   b. God is righteous (2:29)

   c. God is love (4:7)

   d. God is truth and life (5:1, 6, 11, 12, 20)

Therefore, true Christians walk in the light, obey in righteousness and truth, live out love, and have eternal life. The reoccurring themes that depict genuine Christianity are *faith in the truth*, which produces *obedience to God's Word*, which leads to the sacrificial *love of the brethren*.

Chapter 2
The Big Picture

Section I — Prologue:

Christianity is True (Eternal Life is a Reality)—
The Incarnation (1:1-4)

Section II — God is Light

True Christians (Possessors of Eternal Life) Have
Fellowship with the God Who is Light (1:5-2:28)

Section III — God is Righteous

True Christians (Possessors of Eternal Life) Have
Fellowship with the God Who is Righteous
(2:29-4:6)

Section IV — God is Love

True Christians (Possessors of Eternal Life) Have
Fellowship with the God Who is Love (4:7-5:5)

Section V— God is Truth & Life

True Christians (Possessors of Eternal Life) Have
Fellowship with the God Who is Truth and Life
(5:6-21; cf. 5:11-13, 20)

Chapter 3
An Overview Outline

• • • • • •

Section I — Prologue: Christianity is True (Eternal Life is a Reality)—The Incarnation (1:1-4)

Section II — God is Light: True Christians (Possessors of Eternal Life) Have Fellowship with the God Who is Light (1:5-2:28)

I. True Christians (Possessors of Eternal Life) Walk in the Light (1:5-7)

II. True Christians (Possessors of Eternal Life) Confess Sin (1:8-10)

III. True Christians (Possessors of Eternal Life) Have the Ultimate Provision for Sin [and Thus Have Ultimate Victory Over Sin] (2:1-2)

IV. True Christians (Possessors of Eternal Life) Obey Christ's Commandments (2:3-6)

V. True Christians (Possessors of Eternal Life) Love Other Believers (2:7-11)

VI. Be Encouraged: True Christians (Possessors of Eternal Life) Have the Foundation for Victorious Christian Living (2:12-14)

VII. True Christians (Possessors of Eternal Life) Do Not Love the World (2:15-17)

VIII. True Christians (Possessors of Eternal Life) Believe the Truth (2:18-28)

Section III — God is Righteous: True Christians (Possessors of Eternal Life) Have Fellowship with the God Who is Righteous (2:29-4:6)

I. True Christians (Possessors of Eternal Life) Practice Righteousness (2:29)

II. Be Encouraged: True Christians (Possessors of Eternal Life) Have the Promised Hope of Ultimate Righteousness (3:1-3)

III. True Christians (Possessors of Eternal Life) Do Not Practice Sin (3:4-10a)

IV. True Christians (Possessors of Eternal Life) Show Themselves True by Their Love for the Brethren (3:10b-24)

V. True Christians (Possessors of Eternal Life) Can and Must Discern Truth from Error (4:1-6)

Section IV — God is Love: True Christians (Possessors of Eternal Life) Have Fellowship with the God Who is Love (4:7-5:5)

I. True Christians (Possessors of Eternal Life) Are Compelled to Love (4:7-12)

II. Be Encouraged: True Christians (Possessors of Eternal Life) Can Have Assurance of a Personal Relationship with the God Who is Love [Mutual Indwelling] (4:13-19)

III. True Christians (Possessors of Eternal Life) Cannot Separate Love, Faith and Obedience: They Overcome the World (4:20-5:5)

Section V — God is Truth & Life: True Christians (Possessors of Eternal Life) Have Fellowship with the God Who is Truth and Life (5:6-21)

I. True Christians (Possessors of Eternal Life) Believe God's Testimony Concerning His Son (5:6-12)

II. True Christians (Possessors of Eternal Life) Have the Certainty of Eternal Life and Answered Prayer (5:13-17)

III. True Christians (Possessors of Eternal Life) Know the Truth about Their Relationship to Sin, the World, and God Himself (5:18-20)

IV. True Christians (Possessors of Eternal Life) Must Guard Themselves from Idols (5:21)

Chapter 4
A Detailed Outline

Section I — Prologue: Christianity is True (Eternal Life is a Reality)—The Incarnation (1:1-4)

    A. The Proclamation/Message is True (v. 1)

    B. The Person is Real (v. 2)

    C. The Participation/Fellowship is Genuine (v. 3)

    D. The Personal Joy is Unquestionable (v. 4)

Section II — God is Light: True Christians (Possessors of Eternal Life) Have Fellowship with the God Who is Light (1:5-2:28)

I. True Christians (Possessors of Eternal Life) Walk in the Light (1:5-7)

    A. The Foundation of Our Walk (v. 5)

    B. The Folly of Empty Talk (v. 6)

    C. The Freedom of Our Walk (v. 7)

        1. Freedom to Live Out Truth and Holiness

        2. Freedom to Enjoy Fellowship

        3. Freedom to Experience Constant Cleansing

II. True Christians (Possessors of Eternal Life) Confess Sin (1:8-10)

    A. The Definition of Biblical Confession (Ps. 51; Ps. 5)

    B. The Dominant Reason Why We Confess Sin (v. 5, 8b, 10b)

    C. The Description of Those Who Don't Confess Sin (v. 8, 10)

        1. They Deny Sin

        2. They Are Deceived

        3. They Are Void of the Truth

    D. The Description of Those Who Do Confess Sin (v. 9)

        1. They Are Forgiven

        2. They Are Cleansed

E. The Declaration of God's Character to Those Who Confess Sin (v. 9)
   1. He is Faithful
   2. He is Righteous

III. True Christians (Possessors of Eternal Life) Have the Ultimate Provision for Sin [and Thus Have Ultimate Victory Over Sin] (2:1-2)

A. Remember Your Responsibility to Holiness (v. 1a)
B. Remember Your Righteous Defender (v. 1b)
C. Remember Your Righteous Defense (v. 2)

IV. True Christians (Possessors of Eternal Life) Obey Christ's Commandments (2:3-6)

A. The Proof of Fellowship Comes by Obedience (v. 3)
B. The Profession That is False is Exposed by a Lack of Obedience (v. 4)
C. The Perfection of Love Comes by Obedience (v. 5)
D. The Picture of Christ is Displayed by Obedience (v. 6)

V. True Christians (Possessors of Eternal Life) Love Other Believers (2:7-11)

A. We Are Commanded to Love (v. 7, 8)
   1. The Old Command
   2. The New Command
   3. The Biblical Definition of Love
B. We Are Compelled to Love [Because of Who We Are] (v. 8-11)
C. We Are in Contrast to Those Who Walk in Darkness (v. 9-11)

VI. Be Encouraged: True Christians (Possessors of Eternal Life) Have the Foundation for Victorious Christian Living (2:12-14)

A. The Fundamental Foundation (v. 12)
B. The Family Framework of Growth (v. 12-14)
   1. Fathers
   2. Young Men
   3. Children
C. The Founder/Architect/Builder (v. 12-14)

VII. True Christians (Possessors of Eternal Life) Do Not Love the World (2:15-17)

A. Because It is Commanded by God's Word (v. 15a)
B. Because of Our Love for the Father (v. 15b)
C. Because of All That is in the World and Its Opposition to God (v. 16)
   1. The Lust of the Flesh
   2. The Lust of the Eyes
   3. The Pride of Life
D. Because of Our Eternal Perspective (v. 17)

VIII. True Christians (Possessors of Eternal Life) Believe the Truth (2:18-28)

    A. The Reason: Because of Our Anointing from the Holy One (v. 20, 21, 27)

    B. The Results

        1. We Remain In the Fellowship of Believers (v. 18-19)

        2. We Confess Christ (v. 22-23)

        3. We Abide/Remain In the True (Original) Gospel (v. 24)

        4. We Have the Promise of Eternal Life (v. 25)

        5. We Need Not Be Deceived (v. 26-27)

    C. The Responsibility of Believing the Truth (v. 28)

Section III — God is Righteous: True Christians (Possessors of Eternal Life) Have Fellowship with the God Who is Righteous (2:29-4:6)

I. True Christians (Possessors of Eternal Life) Practice Righteousness (2:29)

    A. Because of our Righteous God (v. 29)

    B. Because of Our New Birth (v. 29)

II. Be Encouraged: True Christians (Possessors of Eternal Life) Have the Promised Hope of Ultimate Righteousness (3:1-3)

    A. The Basis of Our Hope: The Father's Love (v. 1)

        1. It Makes Us Children of God

        2. It Makes Us Strangers to the World

    B. The Future Consummation of Our Hope: Christ's Coming (v. 2)

    C. The Present Result of Our Hope: Personal Purification (v. 3)

III. True Christians (Possessors of Eternal Life) Do Not Practice Sin (3:4-10a)

    A. The Reasons (v. 4-9)

        1. Because of What Sin is (v. 4)

        2. Because of What Christ Came To Do and Did (v. 5a, 8b)

        3. Because of Who Christ is (v. 5b, 7)

        4. Because of Our Relationship with Christ (v. 6)

        5. Because of Our New Birth (v. 8a, 9)

    B. The Result: Our Practice Makes It Obvious Who We Belong To (v. 10)

IV. True Christians (Possessors of Eternal Life) Show Themselves True by Their Love for the Brethren (3:10b-24)

    A. It is a Love that Obeys God (v. 10b-12)

    B. It is a Love that is Foreign to This World (v. 13-15)

    C. It is a Love that Sacrifices for Others (v. 16-17)

    D. It is a Love that Shows in the Sincerity of Our Lives (v. 18)

Section V — God is Truth & Life: True Christians (Possessors of Eternal Life) Have Fellowship with the God Who is Truth and Life (5:6-21)

I. **True Christians (Possessors of Eternal Life) Believe God's Testimony Concerning His Son (5:6-12)**

    A. The Testimony of History and the Holy Spirit (v. 6-9)

        1. The Testimony of History: Water and Blood (v. 6)

        2. The Testimony of the Holy Spirit (v. 7-9)

    B. The Internal Testimony of Eternal Life (v. 10)

    C. The Content of God's Testimony (v. 11)

    D. The Verdict (v. 12)

II. **True Christians (Possessors of Eternal Life) Have the Certainty of Eternal Life and Answered Prayer (5:13-17)**

    A. The Certainty of Eternal Life (v. 13)

        1. The Prerequisite

        2. The Promise

    B. The Certainty of Answered Prayer (v. 14-16)

        1. The Promise (v. 14-15)

        2. The Prerequisite (v. 14)

        3. The Picture/Illustration (v. 16b)

        4. The Point of Limitation (v. 16c)

    C. The Certainty of the Seriousness of Sin (v. 17)

III. **True Christians (Possessors of Eternal Life) Know the Truth about Their Relationship to Sin, the World, and God Himself (5:18-20)**

    A. We Are No Longer Friends of Sin (v. 18)

    B. We Are No Longer Citizens of This World (v. 19)

    C. We Are No Longer Estranged from God (v. 20)

IV. **True Christians (Possessors of Eternal Life) Must Guard Themselves from Idols (5:21)**

    A. What is an Idol?

    B. How Can We Guard Ourselves from Idols?

Section One

Prologue:
Christianity is True
Eternal Life is a Reality

The Incarnation
1st John 1:1-4

Chapter 5
Partaking of Eternal Life
• • • • • •

1 John 1:1-4

1) What was from the beginning, what we have heard, what we have seen with our eyes, what we beheld and our hands handled, concerning the Word of Life – 2) and the life was manifested, and we have seen and bear witness and proclaim to you the eternal life, which was with the Father and was manifested to us – 3) what we have seen and heard we proclaim to you also, so that you too may have fellowship with us; and indeed our fellowship is with the Father, and with His Son Jesus Christ. 4) These things we write, so that our joy may be made complete.

    A.   The Proclamation/Message is True (v.1)
    B.   The Person is Real (v. 2)
    C.   The Participation/Fellowship is Genuine (v. 3)
    D.   The Personal Joy is Unquestionable (v. 4)

The Incarnation – Christianity is True [Eternal life is a Reality] (1:1-4)

John presents four encouragements that Christianity is true, so that we would not be deceived, but have fellowship with God. Eternal life is a reality to be enjoyed now and in eternity.

A. The Proclamation/Message is True (v. 1)

Word of Life—

referring to the word about Christ (i.e., the gospel). "What" in verse 1 is literally "that which." It is not "He whom," but "that which." Notice in verse 2, *the life* was manifested, not *the Word*. In this particular context, Christ is the life, not the Word . In John 1:1 and Revelation 19, Jesus is the Word. But here He is the subject of the word, or message (cf. John 11:25; 14:6). It is appropriate to note however, that Jesus is the embodiment of the gospel message. The word about Christ is inextricably bound to the Person of Christ who is the Living Word.

what we have heard —

"we" represents the apostles, who were appointed as witnesses of Christ and the gospel. "Have heard" speaks of the message which John had heard from the Messenger. Jesus is both the Messenger and the Message. "Heard" is not simply past action in the Greek. This was something that had happened in the past and was still having an impact on John's life.

what we have seen with our eyes —

John and the other apostles were both eye and ear witnesses. John physically saw the events we read of in the gospels with his *own eyes*. He personally saw God incarnate – Jesus Christ. Jesus was not a phantom as some of the ancient heretics (and most likely those trying to deceive John's original readers; cf. 4:2-3) taught. Again the Greek grammar indicates lasting effects.

what we beheld —

The Apostle had carefully and deliberately examined the life, Person and events of Christ. First, he lived with Him and learned from Him for three years. Then he looked long at the Lord of glory hanging naked on a tree, suffering for the sins of the world. Then he gazed intently at the risen Christ, before He ascended to heaven in glory.

our hands have handled —

John had personally touched Jesus and leaned on His breast (John 20:27; 21:20; Luke 24:39). He had eaten of the bread and handled the cup at the Last Supper. Such were the things the apostles had heard, seen, beheld, and handled concerning the message of Life.

So John here is verifying the truth of the message by saying, "It's true. Christ and the events of the gospel are fact and reality."

Be encouraged. Not only is the proclamation true, but . . .

B. The Person is Real (v. 2)

All the verbs of verse 1 apply not only to the message about Christ, but to the experience of Christ Himself. He is the message.

The life of God – Jesus Christ was **manifested**, or *made visible, known,* or *clear.* The eternal second Person of the Trinity is the Life who became flesh and dwelt among us as a man.

The glory of the incarnation is that it presents to our adoring gaze not a humanized God or a deified man; but a true God-man—one who is all that God is and at the same time all that man is [yet without sin]; one on whose almighty arm we can rest, and to whose human sympathy we can appeal (B.B. Warfield, quoted in *Benjamin B. Warfield, Selected Shorter Writings,* Vol. 1, edited by John E. Meeter, 1970 pg. 166).

have seen —

in the past, but the effects upon his life were still being experienced. The real events of Jesus' life echoed still in John's memory.

bear witness —

giving ongoing testimony of his Lord based on observation and experience.

proclaim —

means to report on an ongoing basis. The content of John's proclamation is that quality and quantity of life that God possesses without end, which is personified in Christ. John proclaimed Christ as **eternal life**.

who was with the Father —

The grammatical construction of the phrase suggests that Christ, the Eternal Life, was continuously existing in a *face to face*, intimate relationship with God the Father, before the incarnation – and after (cf. 1 John 2:1). Jesus is God (cf. Matt. 11:27). This is the mystery of the Godhead. Jesus is not the Father in identity, but He has existed eternally with Him.

John is saying, "The Person on whom hangs all of Christianity, Jesus Christ, the eternal One is real. I testify to it. It's my business to proclaim it."

Now, after the parenthesis of verse 2, John gets back to grammatically finish the sentence which he began in verse 1. John proclaims to his readers that the *Christian gospel is true* and that *Christ is real,* then he moves to the *purpose* of his announcement which brings us to our third encouragement.

C. The Participation/Fellowship is Genuine [to Those Who Believe the Proclamation] (v. 3)

in order that —

signifies the purpose of John's announcement.

fellowship —

means participation, partaking, partnership. In Luke 5:10, James, John and Peter were said to be *partners* (same word as "fellowship") in the fishing business. Second Peter 1:4 says that Christians have become *partakers* (same word again) of the divine nature. Not that we become little gods, but we become participants in a personal relationship with God Himself (cf. 1 John 3:9). This concept of fellowship forms the basis for the argument of the rest of the book. True Christians manifest the character of the God with whom they have fellowship. How? Through faith in the gospel.

fellowship with <u>us</u> —

this is the apostolic testimony — in other words, the Word of God as fully revealed in the New Testament. Anyone who rejects the testimony of the New Testament rejects true fellowship with God.

And indeed —

John emphasizes the reality of Christian fellowship with the Father and with His Son.

His Son Jesus Christ —

is exploding with theological meaning. The Greek grammar stresses that Jesus is distinct from the Father; yet there is one shared essence with the Father which Christians partake of in fellowship.

Son —

marks out Jesus as the divine Son of God.

Jesus —

is his human name, which means "the Lord is salvation."

Christ —

is the Greek word for Messiah, which means God's anointed King and Deliverer.

So we've been encouraged that the *message is true*, the *Person is real*, the *participation is genuine*, and now –

D. The Personal Joy [for Him Who Shares the Message] is Unquestionable (v. 4)

Here John gives another purpose for his writing.

These things —

most naturally refers to verses 1-3. He was writing of the reality of Christ and the gospel so that his joy could be fulfilled (cf. 2 John 4; 3 John 4).

our joy —

The KJV says "your joy." The NIV and NASB say "our joy." The difference in the Greek is one letter, much like the English. You can see how a scribe could have made the error. It does seem difficult to understand why a scribe would change the more understandable "your joy," to a harder reading of "our joy." Therefore, "our joy" is more likely the original reading. But it is obvious, sharing the gospel with others and partaking of the gospel in faith, that both produce unquestionable joy. John knew that the consummation of his joy would be to share the reality of Christ with his beloved children. Christianity is true. *The message is true. The Person is real. The participation is genuine. And the joy in sharing it is unquestionable.*

Since the message is true – *Do you believe it?*

God the Son came from heaven, took on human form, and died to pay the penalty for the sin by which we have offended a Holy God. He rose from the grave three days later victorious over death and is now exalted at the right hand of the Father in heaven. Have you surrendered your heart to Christ?

Since the message is true – *What are your priorities in life as a Christian?* Are your goals, pursuits and thoughts centered on one thing? Is He your passion and He alone? (Cf. Gal. 6:14)

If the Person of Christ is Real – *Do you trust Him?* Do you take refuge in Jesus the God-man?

If the participation is genuine – *Do you live like it?* Are you growing in holiness, love and faithfulness?

If the personal joy is unquestionable—*Are you sharing your faith and enjoying it?*

John's first assurance to us about the possession of eternal life is that it's true. Christ is eternal life. Be encouraged! Christianity is both true and real. The message of Christ is true and its effect is real and eternal!

True Christians
Possessors of Eternal Life
Have Fellowship with
the God Who is Light

God is Light
1st John 1:5-2:28

Chapter 6
Walking in the Light

• • • • • •

1 John 1:5-7

5) And this is the message we have heard from Him and announce to you, that God is Light, and in Him there is no darkness at all. 6) If we say that we have fellowship with Him and yet walk in the darkness, we lie and do not practice the truth; 7) but if we walk in the Light as He Himself is in the Light, we have fellowship with one another, and the blood of Jesus His Son cleanses us from all sin.

I. **True Christians (Possessors of Eternal Life) Walk in the Light (1:5-7)**

    A.   The Foundation of Our Walk (v. 5)

    B.   The Folly of Empty Talk (v. 6)

    C.   The Freedom of Our Walk (v. 7)

        1.   Freedom to Live Out Truth and Holiness

        2.   Freedom to Enjoy Fellowship

        3.   Freedom to Experience Constant Cleansing

I. True Christians (Possessors of Eternal Life) Walk In the Light (1:5-7)

John's argument is as follows: Since true Christians have fellowship with God (1:3), the God who is light (1:5), genuine Christians therefore, walk in the Light (1:5-7). Our assurance (cf. 5:13) comes as we see our life manifest the character of one born of God. Now in 1:5-7 we will see three truths that will challenge us so that we may know we have eternal life.

A. The Foundation of our Walk (v. 5)

And —

closely connects this section with the prologue of verses 1-4. This is the message that John had heard from **Him** — Christ (cf. verses 1-3). Again, the grammar suggests that the message John had heard so many years previously was still reverberating in his mind.

The message —

which is to follow is in a sense a *summation of the gospel* in terms which we are not normally accustomed to hearing.

John announces to us the truth that Christ revealed: **God is light**. Notice that it does not say "light is God," or "God is a light." God is the Creator of light and uncreated light Himself. *This is a statement about God's nature.* He is Light. John likes to employ this type of terminology (cf. John 4:24; 1 John 4:7-8). This is the foundation of the Christian walk: the character of God. *Every true Christian will manifest, in some measure, the character of his Father.*

We have no biblical record of Jesus saying or teaching these exact words. But remember that Christ is both the Messenger *and the Message*. Hebrews 1:2-3 and John 1 say that Jesus is both the Revealer of God and God Himself. (cf. John 8:12ff; 9:5; 12:35-36, 46; 14:9; Heb. 1:8 and John 14:9). John understood the message. God is Light. Jesus revealed God to be so.

So, true Christians walk in the light because the One with whom they have to do is Light. We are partakers and sharers in the One who is pure light.

But what does it mean that God is Light? Psalm 36:9; 119:105, 130 – *divine truth* (cf. Prov. 6:23; Acts 13:46-47; 26:18, 23; 2 Cor. 4:4-6; 2 Pet. 1:9). Light is knowledge of the truth; darkness is therefore ignorance, falsehood and error. But light in the Scriptures also carries with it a moral quality (cf. Isa. 5:20; Rom. 13:12; Eph. 5:8-13; 1 Thess. 5:4-8). Truth takes action in *holiness*. God is Light. God is *truth and holiness* in His essential being.

See John 3:19-21. True Christians have a foundation rooted in the fact that God is truth and holiness. "[God's] nature as light has an inescapable bearing on the faith and conduct of the believer" (Hiebert, pp. 57-58).

and in Him there is no darkness at all —

"at all" literally means, "not even one bit!" God is totally without stain, blemish or blot. There is not one ounce of falsehood, deception, uncleanness, unholiness, or sin in Him. He is wholly true, and wholly holy.

If God is Light (i.e., truth and holiness), we will manifest truth and holiness. Of course we will never be *truth itself*, or *holiness itself*, because we are created beings. But because God's seed (1 John 3:9) dwells within us, we will manifest His character and live in the light.

True Christians walk in the light. The foundation of their walk is the fact that they have fellowship with the God who is Light.

B. The Folly of Empty Talk (v. 6)

If we say that we have fellowship with Him —

the claim is fellowship with God. This is a claim of Christianity. Yet the one making this claim is walking (present tense) as a continual pattern in darkness.

walk —

is a person's daily conduct of life, in thought and deed—his whole life, inward and outward (Thomas).

darkness —

is emphasized in the original grammar. "In *darkness* we are walking." Darkness is the exact opposite of the nature of God as revealed in verse 5. It is *error, deception, ignorance, impurity and sin*. So, these "professing" Christians are—as an ongoing pattern of life—living in the sphere of "error and sin" (Burdick). Many people call themselves Christians, but the truth is revealed when you find out their view of sin. If sin is biblically defined and mourned over, and considered shameful and painful, then the person likely walks in the light. If sin is denied, or ignored, or excused, or explained away, John characterizes that person as an unbeliever.

lie —

was used outside the New Testament in legal writings to denote a false statement made while under oath (Thomas). "Whenever there is a clear conflict between an individual's 'talk' and his 'walk,' it is always his walk and not his talk that reveals what he really is" (Hiebert, p. 61).

do not practice the truth —

is literally, "do not do the truth." Again, the habitual sense is seen in the Greek.

the truth —

is basically the gospel, even the Word of God.

A person who claims to be a partaker of the divine nature (2 Peter 1:4; i.e., who has "fellowship with God"), and yet is continually walking in sin and living in in contradiction to the Bible and God's holiness — that person is a liar, John says. To call yourself a Christian and yet walk in sin as a pattern of life is folly. What's amazing is that many call themselves Christians, but have no idea what the Bible says about anything, let alone God's holiness and truth (cf. Matthew 7:21-27; 2 Cor. 6:14; James 2:17-20).

C. The Freedom of Our Walk (v. 7)

walk —

is again in the present tense, denoting a pattern of life. This walk is not one of perfection as is clearly seen in 1:9 and 2:1-2, but an overall direction of life.

1. Freedom to Live Out Truth and Holiness

as He Himself is in the light —

Implicit in this statement is the freedom to pursue Christlikeness and godliness.

Believers in Christ are redeemed to be a people zealous for good deeds, created unto good works that God has ordained for them to live out. God is in the sphere of light because He is uncreated light in Himself. Thus we as Christians are free to walk in the light *as He Himself* is in the light (cf. Matt. 5:13-16). Those who are not cleansed by the blood of Christ are enslaved to their sin (c.f. Rom. 6) and not at all free to fulfill the very purpose for which they were created (to love, worship and enjoy God in truth and holiness).

2. Freedom to Enjoy Fellowship

we have fellowship with one another —

Believers have fellowship with other children of God which is ultimately related to fellowship with God. They are free to enjoy the rich rewards and intimacy of those who are sons of the King. They are free to live out eternal life and fellowship to its fullest. If you're walking in the light, you will *not* forsake the assembling together as is the habit of some. But you will congregate and consider how to stimulate one another to love and good deeds (Heb. 10:24-25).

The fellowship of other Christians will be sweet. "He who consistently has trouble maintaining fellowship with others walking in the light should examine his own claim of fellowship with God" (Hiebert, p. 62).

Do you love fellowship? When you get together with other Christians, what does your conversation mostly revolve around?—Christ, redemption, heaven and the hope of glory, love and good deeds? Or the world and the things of the world?—TV, movies, music, sports, money and possessions? I'm not saying we should never talk of these things. I'm asking, "What is our real focus?" The answer will betray where our devotion lies.

Our walk in the light brings freedom to pursue holiness and truth. It brings the freedom of fellowship. And finally it brings . . .

3. The Freedom of Constant Cleansing

the blood —

refers to the infinite sacrifice of Jesus Christ on the cross. Implicitly, the blood represents His perfect and sinless life as a man. Explicitly, it points to His violent death as a substitutionary sacrifice for the sins of mankind. And theologically, the term even encompasses His resurrection from the dead, in which God pronounced victory over death and the satisfaction of His holy wrath poured out upon Christ for all those who would put their faith in Him.

Jesus His Son—

again points to His humanity. A real, literal, flesh-and-bones Man named Jesus shed His blood. But that Man is also God, as pictured by the phrase **His Son.**

cleanses—

The significance of the death of the Son of God is continual **cleansing** from **every kind of sin**. This cleansing is for all who walk in the light, because they are children of the Light, through simple faith in Jesus Christ and His work on the cross. First John 2:12 says believers are forgiven in the past, even with present abiding results. First Corinthians 6:11 says they *were* washed as a completed action. It's done; Christians are washed from sin's power!

Yet 1 John 1:7 presents an ongoing, present cleansing for true Christians. That truth is freedom to pursue righteousness indeed.

Walking in the light exposes the sin that infiltrates a true Christian's life, and Christ's blood immediately purifies and cleanses the child of God. That automatic cleansing is from God's perspective. This is, to be sure, connected with the believer's perspective in verse 9—confession. And 2:1 makes it clear that we do still sin, but sin is no longer the dominating rule in our hearts. And God has made provision—the cleansing blood, the faithful forgiveness and the Righteous Advocate. We are free to press on and pursue Christ—to get up from sin and live out their true heart's desire as a child of God (cf. Ps. 32:1-2, 10-11).

Chapter 7
Confessing Sin

1 John 1:8-10

8) If we say that we have no sin, we are deceiving ourselves and the truth is not in us. 9) If we confess our sins, He is faithful and righteous to forgive us our sins and to cleanse us from all unrighteousness. 10)If we say that we have not sinned, we make Him a liar and His word is not in us.

II. True Christians (Possessors of Eternal Life) Confess Sin (1:8-10)

   A.   The Definition of Biblical Confession (v. 9; Ps. 5; 51)

   B.   The Dominant Reason Why We Confess Sin (v. 5, 8b, 10b)

   C.   The Description of Those Who Don't Confess Sin (v. 8, 10)

   1.   They Deny Sin

   2.   They Are Deceived

   3.   They Are Void of the Truth

   D.   The Description of Those Who Do Confess Sin (v. 9)

   1.   They Are Forgiven

   2.   They Are Cleansed

   E.   The Declaration of God's Character to Those Who Confess Sin (v. 9)

   1.   He is Faithful

   2.   He is Righteous

II. True Christians (Possessors of Eternal Life) Confess Sin (1:8-10)

God's light exposes every imperfection in the lives of Christians. Therefore, we will see in verses 8-10 that true Christians are characterized not only by a life of pursuing holiness, but also of confession of sin, which is made so evident in the light of God's character.

John's argument is as follows: It says in 1:3 that Christians have fellowship with God. And in 1:5 it says that God is light. Since true Christians have fellowship with the God who is light, true Christians walk in the light (1:5-7). A walk in the light of God's truth and holiness exposes sin. Therefore, true Christians confess sin. In 1 John 1:8-10, there are *5 windows into confession of sin* that will help us better understand that those who possess eternal life are marked by their habitual confessing of sin. These should encourage us to confess sin as a part of our daily walk, and as it flows out of our love for God, bring assurance that we possess eternal life.

A. The Definition of Biblical Confession (v.9; Pss. 5, 51).

Confess —

The Greek is actually in the present tense, meaning an ongoing practice. From a biblical perspective, what exactly is confession of sin? The root of the Greek word in verse 9 translated **confess** means *"to say the same thing"* as another – or to agree with another. When "the other" is God, it means that you say the same thing about your sin that God does. Sin is not just a mistake.

What exactly does God say about our sin? Psalm 5:4-5 says: (1) If God takes no pleasure in sin, then we confess that we, as new creatures in Christ, take no pleasure in our sin. (2) Since no evil dwells with God, we as His children agree that this sin should not be in our lives at all. (3) We agree that in our sin we have no right to stand before a holy God. (4) We agree that in our sin we are worthy of the hatred of God, and we agree with God that we too hate our iniquity. This hatred leads us to pursue holiness and victory over that sin through God's power. Though these are not to be used as a ritual for confession or a legalistic guide to confession, we should understand the significance of our sin to a Holy God.

David's prayer in Psalm 51 may be one of the clearest pictures of confession in the Bible. According to Psalm 51:1-3, we are to take personal responsibility for our sin (look at all of the first-person pronouns used). In verse 4, we agree that God has authority, ultimate authority in our lives; we can agree with God that He is right to judge, and we deserve His judgment. In verse 5 we confess that we are sinners by nature. And in verses 7-10, we agree with God that we need Him to cleanse us and change our lives.

In Acts 19:18-20, though in the context of initial confession, the principle still applies that confession involves being specific about our sins (v. 18), and it is inextricably bound to repentance (v. 19). And confession ultimately comes from being confronted with the truth of the Word of God (v. 20). Sin and confession must be defined by God's Word.

B. The Dominant Reason Christians Confess Sin (v. 5, 8b, 10b)

Because **God is light** (v. 5) and we walk in the light as a pattern according to verse 7, we see our need to confess our sin because we are children of light (Eph. 5). *A walk in the light (truth and holiness) exposes any sin.* Though from God's perspective in verse 7, the blood of Jesus is immediately and continually cleansing us; from the human side, when we see our sin in the context of God's light, we confess it to Him.

Not only that, but look at the second half of verse 8. If we say we have no sin, **the truth is not in us**. And in verse 10, those who claim sinlessness make God out to be a liar and **His Word is not in [them]**. *This is tantamount to saying, if you're not a confessor of sin as God defines it, you are not a true Christian* (cf. 1 John 2:20-21).

John's point is crystal clear here in 1 John 1:8-10: unlike some who may claim sinlessness, genuine believers are characterized by the confession of sin because of their fellowship with the God who is Light (see Isaiah 6:1-7 for a graphic illustration of this truth).

The first window in our house of confession exposed the biblical definition of confession. The second window showed us the dominant reason we confess. The third window looks into the filthiest room in the house.

C. The Description of Those Who Don't Confess Sin (v. 8, 10)

1. They Deny Sin

if we say —

introduces another false claim. The first was in verse 6. John again uses "we" in this hypothetical scenario to gently shepherd the flock which may be in contact with such people who make these types of outrageous claims. He addresses the issue in a very pastoral, yet clear way.

we have no sin —

is literally "we are having no sin." This phrase is a denial of the sin principle, of the human sin nature (cf. Ecc. 7:20; Rom. 3:10-12).

In verse 10, the false claim is one of being in a state of sinless perfection. Such people say that they currently stand in the state of not having sinned. They call God a liar (cf. Rom. 3:23).

2. They Are Deceived

First John 1:8 describes people who deny the principle of sin that exists in every man, as self-deceived. The emphasis in the original Greek grammar is on *willful self-deception.* They re-title their sins to make them acceptable in their own minds.

3. They are Void of the Truth

Verse 8 says, **the truth is not in** those who deny their innate sinfulness. The truth of God's Word about Jehovah's redemption of men through Jesus Christ – the gospel – is not in such men. No sin nature, no salvation. That's the description.

In verse 10, those who claim sinless perfection actually call God a liar. People who claim sinlessness are in effect saying God has lied to us about our need for a Savior from our sins. Christ died needlessly, according to them. Again, verse 10 uses slightly different terminology when it says **His word is not in** them. But the result is the same. They are void of God's saving truth – His Word (cf. John 9:41).

D. The Description of Those Who Do Confess Sin (v. 9)

if we confess our sins —

Again, the Greek grammar indicates an ongoing practice. To whom are we to confess? Obviously our confession is to God. In addition, the Bible makes it clear that we are to confess our sins to whomever else was affected by our transgression (cf. Matt. 5:23-25).

Sins —

Notice the plural. We are to be specific in our confession of sins.

1. Forgiven

Confessors, because of God's faithfulness and righteousness, are *forgiven* of their sins and *cleansed* from every unrighteousness. Our obedience to confess does not earn our forgiveness, it expresses it. First John 2:12 says that a Christian has been forgiven (cf. Col. 2:13). A believer can't have unforgiven sins. Jesus paid it all, once and for all time. First John 1:9 says that a true Christian is continually acknowledging and dealing with sin – not in a saving sense but in a communal sense. From a human standpoint, our fellowship can be marred by sin. The promise of confession is forgiveness and cleansing.

to forgive —

means to send away, or dismiss the charges. It means the debt is canceled and taken care of. Possessors of eternal life are characterized by confession of sin because of their relationship to the God who is light. Confessors in turn are described as forgiven.

our sins —

(plural as noted earlier) speaks of individual sins. God uses human terms to describe the absoluteness of His forgiveness. Jeremiah 31:34 says that when God forgives, the issue is no longer remembered. Isaiah 44:22 says it is no longer seen. Micah 7:19 calls the offense dead and irretrievable. These descriptions are figures of speech and should not be taken in a woodenly literal fashion.

2. Cleansed

to cleanse —

is to purify from the stain and pollution of sin. (Cf. Isa. 1:18 - purity from the stain of unrighteousness.) Being cleansed from both the result and even the cause of sin is a wonderful treasure for the believer. For the unbeliever it is a matter of envy since this is the very object of his quest for righteousness through religious activity. But God's Word declares it to be a gift.

from all unrighteousness —

means we're cleansed from every kind of failure to measure up to the standard of what is right as defined by God in His Word (cf. Isa. 6:5-7; Luke 23:39-43; Rev. 7:13-14). How are we forgiven and cleansed? First John 1:7 and 2:1-2 say the blood of Christ is the only means of forgiveness and cleansing in all the world.

E. The Declaration of God's Character to Those Who Confess Sin (v. 9)

1. He is Faithful

God is loyal to His promises in Scripture to forgive the sins of those who repent and believe the Lord Jesus Christ. He is consistent and completely trustworthy. Donald Burdick said it well:

The foundation upon which the assurance of forgiveness rests is indicated in these two attributes of God. His faithfulness and righteousness are not dependent on confession. Instead, upon confession He is found to be faithful and righteous (Burdick, p. 126).

Notice the comforting promise God gives to Israel concerning His eternal, unchangeable character—Isaiah 40:8—"The grass withers, the flower fades, but the word of our God stands forever." Remember the words of Joshua to Israel near the end of his life: "Now behold, today I am going the way of all the earth, and you know in all your hearts and in all your souls that not one word of all the good words which the LORD your God spoke concerning you has failed; all have been fulfilled for you, not one of them has failed" (Josh. 23:14). It's the same for us today. Jesus said in His high priestly prayer to the Father, "Thy Word is truth" (John 17:17). Be encouraged. The God whose Word is truth, Who cannot lie, Who is light and in Him there is no darkness at all— this One has promised to forgive us and cleanse us. And God's Word never fails.

2. He is Righteous

We might have expected John to say that God is "merciful" in forgiving our sins; although true, that would have been less assuring to our troubled hearts. Conscious of our persistent failures, we might come to fear that God would say, "Your sinning no longer deserves my merciful forgiveness." But the declaration that He is righteous reminds us that in forgiving our sins God acts in full moral consistency with His character in view of the cross (Hiebert, p. 66).

God doesn't unjustly let the guilty go free. He is not like a corrupt judge who looks the other way when criminals admit their crime. If you saw a judge free the man who harmed your family, you would be outraged at the injustice. With God there is no such injustice. He is Light and in Him is no darkness at all. First John 2:29 says that He is righteous. God is always and ever, completely right and righteous in everything He is and does. So how can He be righteous in forgiving guilty sinners like you and me (cf. 2 Cor. 5:21; Rom. 3:21-26)? God in Christ paid the just penalty for our sins against Him. He can righteously forgive those who run to Him in faith because Jesus paid the debt. He showed His approval of Christ's substitution when He raised Him from the grave. Because Christ lives, so shall all those live who trust in Him alone for their forgiveness, cleansing, and very life.

If you want a picture of God's faithfulness and righteousness to forgive sins, look no further than the Cross. At the Cross He was faithful to His very first promise of redemption in Genesis 3:15. At the Cross He was righteous to carry out the just wages of sin, death. The ultimate picture is of the Creator, Jesus Christ the God-man, suffering for His own creatures' sins—then risen triumphant from the grave, where death could no longer hold Him. **If we confess our sins, He is faithful and righteous to forgive us our sins, and cleanse us from all unrighteousness.**

But don't be deceived. False teachers will tell you that you don't have to confess sin or walk in the light. Or else they'll tell you that the blood of Christ doesn't cleanse you from *all* your sins. They'll in effect tell you that God is not truly faithful to cleanse you from *all* your iniquity, and that you must participate in the prescribed works of their religious system to be saved. But God *is* faithful and righteous. Christ *is* enough and all you need.

Chapter 8
Having an Advocate
• • • • • •

1 John 2:1-2

1) My little children, I am writing these things to you that you may not sin. And if anyone sins, we have an Advocate with the Father, Jesus Christ the righteous; 2) and He Himself is the propitiation for our sins; and not for ours only, but also for those of the whole world.

III. **True Christians (Possessors of Eternal Life) Have the Ultimate Provision for Sin [and Thus Have Ultimate Victory Over Sin] (2:1-2)**

    A. Remember Your Responsibility to Holiness (v. 1a)

    B. Remember Your Righteous Defender (v. 1b)

    C. Remember Your Righteous Defense (v. 2)

III. Be Encouraged: True Christians (Possessors of Eternal Life) Have the Ultimate Provision for Sin [A Righteous Defender and Righteous Defense] (2:1-2)

In light of the ongoing battle with sin, and the seemingly never-ending cycle of confession and repentance, John in 1 John 2:1-2 reminds his readers of their *ultimate provision* for sin which gives them victory. Then he balances that comforting truth with the issue of obedience to God's Word in 2:3-6.

The apostle gives three exhortations in light of God's ultimate provision for sin.

A. Remember Your Responsibility to Holiness (v. 1a)

My little children —

> this very first phrase is a term of endearment and comfort meant to encourage John's readers. It is a pastoral term that is meant to soften the blow of such a high standard of not sinning at all. He is careful in light of the forgiveness in 1:9, to remind his readers that sin is not to be indulged in because grace abounds (cf. Rom. 6:1).

these things —

> refers to what he has written previously in chapter 1. God is light. His children do walk in the light. Those who walk in darkness—those who deny sin—are deceived and void of God's saving truth.

may not sin—

> The immediate purpose of John's writing these things is **that you may not sin**. Romans 6:12-18 and 1 Corinthians 10:13 say that we are no longer enslaved to sin. We have a new nature. We can overcome. The Bible says an unbeliever is a slave to sin. But as Christians, we do not have to sin. John's goal and desire for us is the elimination of not just the habitual patterns of sin in our lives, but *every* sinful thought, word and deed. And one day, when we are glorified, we will fulfill that goal. For now, we are to pursue what one day we shall be.

B. Remember Your Righteous Defender (v. 1b)

And —

> John used the normal word for "and" to tell his readers that not only is he writing them to urge them to holiness, but also to comfort them concerning sin and the fact that God has made the ultimate provision for it.

If anyone sins —

> this is potential or possible, not mandatory or necessary. "If anyone of us should sin," is the idea. Remember, Scripture commands us not to sin. John has just exhorted us not to sin. But "if anyone sins" – according to the Greek, this is an *act of sin*, not a habitual lifestyle of unrepentant sin (cf. v. 6).

we have an Advocate —

> John includes himself here with all Christians as having an advocate.

Advocate —

> means one called along side to help. It is legal terminology, but not of a professional lawyer trying to get his client off the hook by sidestepping justice. An advocate provides intercessory type of legal assistance. He is a personal defender, not a professional one. He is the friend who comes before the judge pleading on behalf of the defendant. In that sense, an advocate can rightly be called a "defender." Jesus is our personal Defender, in our case, before a Holy God.

with the Father —

> again, the word translated "with" has the root meaning of "facing." We have a personal Advocate who has a face-to-face relationship with the Father (1 John 1:2; Rom. 8:34; Heb. 7:23-25; 8:1-2).

Jesus —

> refers to Christ in His humanity. Our Defender is a man. Therefore he can intercede on behalf of men.

Christ —

> is a reference to Jesus as the Divine King and Annointed Redeemer. Jesus Christ, our advocate is the God-man—the King who knows the Father face to face, who came to set us free.

righteous —

> Amazingly, our Defender is righteous. He is perfectly right in all that He is by character and quality – and all that He says, does, and decrees. He who pleads the Christian's case is always right and righteous in His character—even as God is righteous—because He is God. He is our Defender against the accuser (Rev. 12:10). Jesus Christ the Righteous is our Advocate/High Priest (Rom. 8:33-34; Heb. 4:12-16; Zech. 3:1-5). Romans 3:26 reminds us that God is a just justifier.

C. Remember Your Righteous Defense (v. 2)

Not only is Christ our righteous Defender, He is our righteous Defense.

He Himself —

> Our personal Advocate doesn't just plead our case. Emphatically, *He is* our case.

propitiation —

satisfactory or adequate sacrifice for the averting of divine wrath. Christ is the sufficient sacrifice. God's offended holiness must be propitiated – satisfied. A good judge must and will judge sin (Rom. 3:23-26; Nahum 1:3; Deut. 32:4; 2 Cor. 5:21). Christ *is* — not was — but is (present tense) the satisfaction concerning God's holiness that we have offended as sinners. We trust Christ for our forgiveness and righteousness. He is our *only* Defense. He is the *only* acceptable sacrifice that will avert the righteous wrath of God against us. His death is of infinite value because He is the God-man. And only that death of infinite value can satisfy an infinitely Holy God (Heb. 9:11-14, 22-28; Heb. 7:22-27). And now, through the resurrection, He ever lives to intercede for us as our Defender and Defense.

First John 2:2b says, **not concerning our sins only, but also concerning those of the whole world.**

for —

in this context means "concerning or pertaining to." This verse does not mean that all sinners will go to heaven when they die regardless of their faith and lives. Jesus didn't effectually substitute for every person who ever lived. If that were the case, everyone would go to heaven and no one would ever go to hell. That's called universalism. The Bible obviously does not teach that (Rev. 21:7-8). Though Christ's sacrifice is infinitely sufficient to atone for all of the sins of all the people of all the ages, God's effectual atonement is limited only to those who call out in faith to the Lord Jesus Christ (John 3:36) — the elect from before the foundation of the earth (Eph. 1).

Those who don't obey Christ will be thrown into eternal judgment, the Lake of Fire (Rev. 21). What does this verse mean then? John is saying that for all of lost humanity (not just an elite few with special knowledge, as the Gnostic heretics taught) there is no other satisfactory sacrifice for sin to avert the judgment of God, except Jesus Christ. The sacrificial death and shed blood of Jesus Christ was the *only* acceptable, God-appeasing sacrifice that could have been offered to a holy God. There are not many paths to God. Jesus is the only way.

Chapter 9
Obeying Christ's Commandments

●●●●●●

1 John 2:3-6

3) By this we know that we have come to know Him, if we keep His commandments. 4) The one who says, "I have come to know Him," and does not keep His commandments, is a liar, and the truth is not in him; 5) but whoever keeps His word, in him the love of God has truly been perfected. By this we know that we are in Him: 6) the one who says he abides in Him ought himself to walk in the same manner as He walked.

IV. True Christians (Possessors of Eternal Life) Obey Christ's Commandments (2:3-6)

    A. The Proof of Fellowship Comes by Obedience (v. 3)

    B. The Profession that is False is Exposed by a Lack of Obedience (v. 4)

    C. The Perfection of Love Comes by Obedience (v. 5)

    D. Picture of Christ is Displayed by Obedience (v. 6)

IV. True Christians (Possessors of Eternal Life) Obey Christ's Commandments (2:3-6)

Here the apostle John gives four truths explaining the relationship between obedience and true Christianity.

A. The Proof of Fellowship Comes by Obedience (v. 3)

by this —

refers to the following thought —"if we keep His commandments." Notice he says, **By this we** *know*, not "By this we become in Him, or, "by this we are saved." But, "by this we know." We ascertain or acquire knowledge about and establish our certainty about our relationship with Him. We come to recognize that we are in Him. An interpretive translation would be as follows: "By this we are coming to recognize that we have come to know Him (in the past with present abiding results), if we keep His commandments."

If —

is not a condition to know Him, it is a condition to recognize the fact that we do know Him (see Burdick, p. 132).

come to know Him —

talks of a personal relationship.

Him —

most naturally refers to Christ in 2:1, yet remember Christ is God in the flesh (Col. 2:9; John 10). We have a personal relationship with God through Christ. And notice the text says, "we have come to know Him", not "we have come to know about Him." (Burdick, p. 135). This is the test that proves the reality of our relationship with God — **if we keep His commandments**.

keep —

speaks of watchful care, both externally and internally. This is heart obedience, not just external compliance. It is in the *present tense*, which means this watchful care is a way of life. The habit or pattern of this person's life is obedience to Christ's commandments.

commandments —

not the Ten Commandments or the Mosaic law. John uses a different word in John 1:17, 46 when he refers to the "law" of Moses. Here "commandment" means simply the Bible – God's will – the Word of God (cf. John 14:15, 21, 23-24).

First John 2:3 says that the proof of fellowship with God comes by a pattern of heart and life obedience to God's Word. We know he's not talking about sinless perfection because of 1:7, 8-10; 2:1-2, but definitely the grammar clearly speaks of a pattern or lifestyle of obedience. True knowledge *of* God (not just head knowledge *about* God) produces a heart to obey.

B. The Profession that is False is Exposed by a Lack of Obedience (v. 4)

I have come to know Him—

The claim is one of ongoing, abiding fellowship with God. This is a claim that one has become a Christian. But the reality of this person's life is that he has a habitual pattern of no real heart obedience to God's Word. Not only is this person's statement a lie — God's Word here in verse 4 calls him a liar. He is a liar in his character. This person does not possess the truth.

truth —

is the saving revelation/principle that comes from God and His Word. (In some places the truth is God's Word [John 17:17], or Jesus Himself [John 14:6], or even a principle that sets men free [John 8:32]). No matter what anyone may claim, if there is not a life that is seeking to grow in obedience to God's Word, there is no proof of a relationship with God. No one, no matter what he may say about knowing Christ or being a Christian, who has no desire to know God's Word — the Bible — can be assured he has eternal life. In fact, God's Word challenges him and calls him a liar.

The proof of our fellowship comes by obedience. The profession that is false is exposed by disobedience. In verse 5, we see the result of obedience.

C. The Perfection of Love comes by Obedience (v. 5)

But —

in contrast to the liar or the false professor.

whoever —

anyone (unrestricted) who is keeping (present tense) —not just externally, but from the heart — Christ's Word, the love of God has truly been perfected.

Notice, John uses the term **word** in v. 5 in the same sense that he used "commandments" in v. 3-4. He meant the same thing: namely, the Bible — God's Word.

truly —

There is an emphasis on the word **truly** in the Greek. In contrast to the false claim of verse 4, the obedient one is actually a conduit for perfecting God's love.

the love of God —

could mean either God's love, or our love for God. In light of 1 John 4:19, we know that we love only because God first loved us. In a sense, our love ultimately stems from God's love.

How can God's love be perfected? The term "is perfected" means to fulfill its mission, or reach its intended goal (Burdick, p. 138). In other words, God's love comes to its intended goal when we obey His Word. Walking in obedience to His Word is not only the right way, but the very best, most loving, and joyous way to live.

Verse 5 ends by restating that knowing we are in Christ comes by obedience — which results from God's love in our lives.

D. The Picture of Christ is Seen by Obedience (v. 6)

the one who says —

This is the same grammatical construction as v. 4. These words introduce a claim that can be tested. Verse 4 clearly speaks of false professors. Verse 6 is simply a statement of fact. Again, the claim is one of continued abiding in Christ. This is a claim of intimacy with God.

ought —

morally, spiritually and logically obligated. The one claiming fellowship with God is internally compelled to walk in the same manner as He walked.

He —

is literally, "that One." It obviously refers to Jesus and His life here as a man in the midst of humanity.

How did Christ walk?

- In sacrificial love (John 13:12-17)
- In suffering and trials (1 Pet. 2:21-23)
- As a Servant (Mark 10:45)
- Knowing and using the Word of God (Matt. 4:1-4)
- Striving against sin (Matt. 4)
- With humility and gentleness (Matt. 11:29)
- With a passion for evangelism (Luke 19:10)
- In obedience (John 4:24)
- In prayer (Mark 1:35)
- In submission (Heb. 5:7; Matt. 26:39)

Chapter 10
Loving the Brethren
● ● ● ● ● ●

1 John 2:7-11

7) Beloved, I am not writing a new commandment to you, but an old commandment which you have had from the beginning; the old commandment is the word which you have heard. 8) On the other hand, I am writing a new commandment to you, which is true in Him and in you, because the darkness is passing away, and the true light is already shining. 9) The one who says he is in the light and yet hates his brother is in the darkness until now. 10) The one who loves his brother abides in the light and there is no cause for stumbling in him. 11) But the one who hates his brother is in the darkness and walks in the darkness, and does not know where he is going because the darkness has blinded his eyes.

V. True Christians (Possessors of Eternal Life) Love Other Believers (2:7-11)

    A. We Are Commanded to Love (v. 7, 8)
        1. The Old Command
        2. The New Command
        3. The Biblical Definition of Love
    B. We Are Compelled to Love [Because of Who We Are] (v. 8-11)
    C. We Are Set in Contrast to Those Who Walk in Darkness (v. 9-11)

V. True Christians (Possessors of Eternal Life) Love Their Brothers (2:7-11)

A. We Are Commanded to Love (v. 7, 8)

The context of verses 9-11 points to love as the summation of the commandment (note that commandment is singular, in contrast to v. 3).

Beloved —

a term of endearment. In one word, John is pointing out that his readers are recipients of both his love and divine love. From this first word, John draws attention to the theme of love.

1. The Old Command (v. 7)

This command to love is not some strange new gospel teaching just invented by the apostle.

not writing a new commandment —

this was not a new *kind* of command (unlike the kind of teaching the deceivers of 2:26 were most likely involved in).

But —

denotes a strong contrast.

old —

must be defined contextually. It is the **commandment which you have had from the beginning** or literally, "which you were having from the beginning." In other words, the command to love was an essential part of the gospel which they first heard and were hearing (note the end of verse 7, "the commandment is the word *which you have heard*"; cf. 3:11).

2. The New Command (v. 8)

On the other hand —

literally, "again." This phrase connects the thought of verse 7 to verse 8, but gives a different vantage point.

new —

this command is qualitatively new.

which —

Christ obeyed the command to love. He loved His brothers all the way to death. John's readers were in the process of living out God's love. In a sense, the new command is—live it—experience sacrificial love, then choose to love with your life. Live the old command in a new way—the way Jesus lived it (cf. John 13:34).

***true* —**

> the newness of the command is a *reality* in Christ and in believers **because** the **darkness** (the realm of error with the moral quality of evil) is **passing away** (even now) and the **true light** (genuine truth and moral holiness) is **already** (now) **shining**.

3. What is Biblical Love?

- humble service/humility - John 13:34-35
- self-emptying/humiliation -Philippians 2:1-8
- sacrifice of one's own life - John 15:12
- takes action and makes provision - 1 John 3:17
- unsolicited and not for personal gain - 1 John 4:10
- seeking to obey the Bible in every situation and relationship - 2 John 5-6
- a choice that *gives* of oneself - John 3:16
  (See also 1 Corinthians 13)

> This is the kind of love we are commanded to live out.

B. We Are Compelled to Love Because of Who We Are

> Verse 9 is yet another false claim of fellowship.

***the one who hates* —**

> this is a present tense/habitual attitude which would include indifference and is the opposite of biblical love (cf. above). Those who don't sacrificially love other believers ("his brother") are not true Christians ("in the darkness"; cf. 1 John 1:5-7).

***the one who loves* —**

> again the present tense/habitual attitude of humble, sacrificial action toward other believers.

***abides* —**

> literally, "is abiding" or remaining/dwelling.

> Other Scriptures command love for enemies and neighbors, which constitute everyone (cf. Matt. 5:44; 19:19; Luke 6:27). But here the command is to love others who are born of God. This limited use is significant. A test of the

genuineness of your claim of being a Christian can be seen in whether or not you sacrificially love other Christians. True Christians are compelled to love because they have fellowship with God (cf. 5:1). God lives in them.

and there is no cause for stumbling in him —

as we are living in the light we see clearly the truth of God. There is nothing within the sphere of light (in which we are walking) to cause us to stumble. Walking in love defends us against falling into sin (cf. 2 Pet. 1:5-10; Gal. 5:13, 14, 22-23).

C. We Are Set in Contrast to Those in Darkness (v. 9-11; see also Proverbs 4:19)

Verse 9 —

those who are not loving other Christians (i.e., hating) are in darkness until now, but a true Christian walks in the light (1:5-7). Verses 10-11 also expose the contrast between those in the light and those in darkness.

These verses (9-11) are not talking about sometimes falling into this sin of hate (cf. 1:8-2:2). One of the tensions of the Christian life is to see the lack of love in your life and yet long for and strive for holiness (cf. Rom. 7). Let 1 John 2:1-2 be our comfort.

Verse 11 —

the one who is *habitually hating* (present tense) is in the darkness and is walking (present tense) in the sphere of darkness (error and impurity).

and does not know where he is going —

this phrase marks this false professor off as completely lost and sets him in contrast to a true Christian. Jesus used the same wording in John 12:35-36. The sons of the light are heading to the kingdom of light.

because the darkness has blinded his eyes —

an unbeliever does not know where he is going because the error and impurity of his ways have blinded his eyes. His walk in darkness is a stumbling block in contrast to the one described in verse 10.

Chapter 11
Being Forgiven

●●●●●●

1 John 2:12-14

12) I am writing to you, little children, because your sins have been forgiven you for His name's sake. 13) I am writing to you, fathers, because you know Him who has been from the beginning. I am writing to you, young men, because you have overcome the evil one. I have written to you, children, because you know the Father. 14) I have written to you, fathers, because you know Him who has been from the beginning. I have written to you, young men, because you are strong, and the word of God abides in you, and you have overcome the evil one.

VI. Be Encouraged: True Christians (Possessors of Eternal Life) Have the Foundation for Victorious Christian Living (2:12-14)

    A. The Fundamental Foundation (v. 12)

    B. The Family Framework of Growth (v. 12-14)

        1. Fathers

        2. Young Men

        3. Children

    C. The Founder/Architect/Builder (v. 12-14)

VI. Be Encouraged: True Christians (Possessors of Eternal Life) Have the Foundation For Victorious Christian Living (2:12-14)

After spelling out the uncompromising standards of obedience to God's Word and Christ-like love for the brethren, John gives his readers some pastoral encouragement to contrast with the hard condemnation he has given false professors of the faith. It's as if John thought, "I've just told them that true Christians obey Christ's Word, so they ought to walk according to the perfect standard of Christ. They must love other Christians like Christ loved. I've told them that those who don't live this way are not really Christians at all. And I'm about ready to command them not to love the world or the things of the world. So I'd better encourage these dear little ones and remind them of the basis for a victorious Christian life. They *can* live these things out. In contrast to those in darkness (v. 11), I trust they do know God. They are forgiven. They can have victory—every one of them from the youngest in the faith to the most mature."

A. The Fundamental Foundation (v. 12)

little children —

cf. 2:1, 28

forgiven —

The grammar denotes a completed action in the past with present, abiding results (cf. Col 2:13-14; Acts 10:43). We are permanently released from the legal, and progressively the behavioral grip of sin on us.

for His name's sake —

This is the basis for our complete forgiveness. "His" is referring to Christ. "Name's sake" theologically means "because of Christ's Person as the God-Man" — His life, substitutionary/atoning death, and resurrection from the dead. In other words, a Christian's completed forgiveness is not on his own merit, but solely because of who Jesus is and what He has done to accomplish our redemption and forgiveness. It is because of Christ that men are forgiven, through faith in His name.

Remember the meaning of biblical forgiveness (Jer. 31:34; Isa. 44:22; Micah 7:19; Ps. 103:12). God declares us forgiven on the basis of Christ's merit, not our own (Rom. 8:1-2). Our justification (being declared righteous by God on the basis of faith in Christ) and our understanding of it is fundamental and vital to our progressive sanctification (growth in daily, practical holiness). God's mercy and forgiveness and the hope to come cause us to delight in God and thus pursue obedience to His Word.

Victorious Christian living is rooted in the understanding of the forgiveness of sins.

B. The Family Framework of Growth (v. 12-14)

All of the following categories are in some measure true of all believers. Yet John applies them specifically to certain groups of Christians according to the different stages of maturity in the faith.

1. Fathers

fathers —

It is the *spiritually mature* who prize Christ and walk with Him in the most consistent way (cf. Phil. 3:7-10; 2 Tim. 1:12 "know").

Him who has been from the beginning —

Christ (cf. 1 John 1:1).

All genuine believers know (personally and intimately) Christ. This is a fundamental truth of Christianity. But as stated earlier, in general the mature believers experience a more consistent communion with their Lord.

2. Young Men

young men —

growing and doctrinally sound believers. Again, all believers have overcome the world (1 John 5:4-5; 2 Cor. 4:4), but those who are strong in the Word of God experience practical victory over the evil one and his corrupt system. Victory over sin is directly related to the true knowledge of the Word of God (cf. Ps. 119:9-11; 2 Tim. 3:15-17; James 1:21-22ff).

Note the correlation between Ephesians 5:18ff and Colosians 3:16ff.

3. Children

children —

this is a different Greek word than is used in verse 12. The term means a young one who is under the authority of another. Metaphorically it can mean one who is spiritually young.

Scripture says that God is the enemy of the unbeliever (Rom. 5:10; Col. 1:21). But the believer now has God as his Father by new birth (see John 3; 1 Peter 1:3-5) and adoption (Eph. 1; Rom. 8:14-16). As children and sons of God we are heirs. We have an inheritance because God is our Father (Eph. 1:18-19; 1 John 3:1-3; 1 Pet. 1:3-5).

C. The Founder/Architect/Builder

for His name's sake —

God in Christ (see above note).

Him who has been from the beginning —

Christ who is eternal life Himself.

the Father —

God the Father.

the word of God —

authored and given by God the Holy Spirit.

The *foundation* of victorious Christian living is the complete forgiveness of our sins in Christ. The *framework* for victorious Christian living is growth in spiritual maturity and the knowledge of God. The *Founder* and *Builder* of victorious Christian living is the Triune God—Father, Son and Holy Spirit.

Chapter 12
Not Loving the World

••••••

1 John 2:15-17

15) Do not love the world nor the things in the world. If anyone loves the world, the love of the Father is not in him. 16) For all that is in the world, the lust of the flesh and the lust of the eyes and the boastful pride of life, is not from the Father, but is from the world. 17) The world is passing away, and also its lusts; but the one who does the will of God lives forever.

VII. True Christians (Possessors of Eternal Life) Do Not Love the World (2:15-17)

   A.   Because It is Commanded by God's Word (v. 15a)

   B.   Because of Our Love for the Father (v. 15b)

   C.   Because of All That is in the World and Its Opposition to God (v. 16)

       1.   The Lust of the Flesh

       2.   The Lust of the Eyes

       3.   The Pride of Life

   D.   Because of Our Eternal Perspective (v. 17)

VII. True Christians (Possessors of Eternal Life) Do Not Love the World (2:15-17)

After encouraging his readers about the forgiveness of their sins, intimacy with God, sonship and victory, the Apostle John now turns to an exhortation against the love of the world.

First John 2:15-17 gives four reasons true Christians do not, and should not love the world system.

A. Because It is Commanded by God's Word (v. 15a)

Do not love —

this is an imperative/command. It is commanded by the God of the universe. The God who sent His Son to redeem us from our sins commands it. The God who came as a man and suffered and died for our sin commands it. The God who gave us His Word by His Spirit commands it.

Notice that He does not command us to remove ourselves from the world and become hermits or monks. In fact, in John 17:14-18 Jesus prays to sanctify believers and send them into the world as lights for Him.

love —

this term encompasses the ideas of setting your affections upon and sacrificially living for the object of your love. It stems from a "steady devotion of the will" (Stott, p. 99).

True Christians *do not* habitually and persistently love the world, but sometimes we do flirt with it. John's command is to constantly be on guard against loving the world. If you have fallen into it, stop it—because it is inconsistent with the character of God and with a child of God's new nature.

world —

in Scripture there are three different usages of this specific Greek term:

- the earth or creation in Acts 17:24
- the human race in general as image bearers of God, as in John 3:16 (cf. Matt. 5:43-48)
- the evil system that is opposed to God and His righteousness, as in 1 John 2:16; 3:1; 4:4; 5:4, 19; John 12:31.

Verse 16 makes it clear in context that "world" is the evil system that is opposed to God. So the world, which we are not to love, is everything this present, evil, God-opposing system throws in our faces every day. Satan is the ruler of this age and the things of this world.

things of the world —

verse 16 defines this term as it relates to the attitudes and desires of men (i.e., the lusts of the flesh, etc.).

B. Because of Our Love for the Father (v. 15b)

love of the Father —

> this expression can either mean "the Father's love," or "love for the Father." Because of the immediate context (it is set in contrast with love *for* the world), it most likely refers to "love *for* the Father." But either way the result is the same (cf. 1 John 4:19).

If anyone loves —

> the verb "loves" is present tense, indicating an ongoing/habitual loving of the world.

not in him —

> love for God is not in the man who is consistently devoted to the world, or to the things in the world, no matter what he may claim about being a Christian or having fellowship with God.

> A man whose life is characterized by a steady devotion to the God-hating world system shows that he has no real love for God the Father. Love for God and love for the world and its things are "mutually exclusive" (Stott, p. 99).

C. Because of All That is in the World and Its Opposition to God (v. 16)

all that is in the world —

> is further defined by three categories. Again, note the negative emphasis on the attitudes of men toward things. The "things" or material objects themselves are not necessarily bad (cf. Col. 2:8).

1. Lust of the Flesh

lust —

> a passionate desire; the expression is usually used with an evil connotation, but occasionally can also refer in Scripture to a good desire (cf. Luke 22:15; 1 Thess. 2:17).

of the flesh —

> desires springing from the flesh (Burdick, p. 179).

flesh —

The Bible makes it clear that the body isn't evil in and of itself (1 Cor. 6:13ff). In this context, it is our propensity toward evil and the principle of sin that exists in our fallen humanity (cf. Rom. 8:12-13).

What are some lusts of the flesh that the world promotes? The world promotes sexual immorality, alcohol abuse, drug abuse, etc. These are some of the most obvious ones, but how about gluttony and gossip, or the inordinate desire for comfort and the life of ease. [Laziness, oversleeping, prayerlessness, and a lack of spiritual discipline can also be categorized as lusts of the flesh.] See also Genesis 3:6 (good for food).

2. Lust of the Eyes

The passionate desires created *by* what is seen, and *for* what is seen. The desire for worldly beauty (billboards, magazines, TV, movies, sports, etc.) can be an opportunity for the lust of the eyes, if we do not guard our hearts, think critically and avoid temptation. Again, see Genesis 3:6 (saw/delight to the eyes) and Matthew 4:8-9.

3. Pride of Life

That boastful pride and desire to be exalted, to have control, and to get "what I want." Yet again, Genesis 3:4-6 (you will be like God/desirable to make one wise) and Matthew 4:5-7. (Don't forget religious pride.)

How can a believer respond to these temptations of the world (I Cor. 10:13)? Christ answered the devil with specific, applicable Scriptures (cf. Matt. 4). Colosians 3:16 is always helpful. Notice also Hebrews 11:24-29. *By faith* Moses refused/consciously opposed the pride of life (v. 24), chose to deny the lust of the flesh (v. 25), considered the value of heaven as greater than the lust of the eyes (v. 26-27). *Faith* - acting on and according to the truth of God's Word, not living according to circumstance, emotions, feelings, or impulses.

D. Because of Our Eternal Perspective (v. 17)

passing away —

> currently, even now the world system opposed to God is in the process of *disintegrating*. God's Word says that in reality all these things that seem so attractive and tempting are actually falling apart—they will not last and can never satisfy.

but —

> the contrast is clear. You cannot have both.

the one who does —

> present tense/habitual practice of life. "It is this resolute obedience, imperfect though it may be, that brings the assurance of permanence amid the present scene of change and decay" (Hiebert, p. 104).

the will of God —

> God's will is revealed in the Bible (cf. Ps. 41:8; 119:1ff).

abides forever —

> eternal dwelling/abiding with God (cf. Rev. 21-22).

> See the encouragement of 1 John 5:4-5 and John 16:33. Press on and fight the good fight of faith because Jesus has paid it all, conquered death, sin and hell— and won the victory.

Chapter 13
Believing the Truth
● ● ● ● ● ●

1 John 2:18-28

18) Children, it is the last hour; and just as you heard that antichrist is coming, even now many antichrists have appeared; from this we know that it is the last hour. 19) They went out from us, but they were not really of us; for if they had been of us, they would have remained with us; but they went out, in order that it might be shown that they all are not of us. 20) But you have an anointing from the Holy One, and you all know. 21) I have not written to you because you do not know the truth, but because you do know it, and because no lie is of the truth. 22) Who is the liar but the one who denies that Jesus is the Christ? This is the antichrist, the one who denies the Father and the Son. 23) Whoever denies the Son does not have the Father; the one who confesses the Son has the Father also. 24) As for you, let that abide in you which you heard from the beginning. If what you heard from the beginning abides in you, you also will abide in the Son and in the Father. 25) This is the promise which He Himself made to us: eternal life. 26) These things I have written to you concerning those who are trying to deceive you. 27) As for you, the anointing which you received from Him abides in you, and you have no need for anyone to teach you; but as His anointing teaches you about all things, and is true and is not a lie, and just as it has taught you, you abide in Him. 28) Now, little children, abide in Him, so that when He appears, we may have confidence and not shrink away from Him in shame at His coming.

VIII.   True Christians (Possessors of Eternal Life) Believe the Truth (2:18-28)

      A.   The Reason: Because of Our Anointing from the Holy One (v. 20, 21, 27)

      B.   The Results

          1.   We Remain In the Fellowship of Believers (v. 18-19)

          2.   We Confess Christ (v. 22-23)

          3.   We Abide/Remain In the True (Original) Gospel (v. 24)

4. We Have the Promise of Eternal Life (v. 25)
5. We Need Not Be Deceived (v. 26-27)
C. The Responsibility of Believing the Truth (v. 28)

F. True Christians (Possessors of Eternal Life) Believe the Truth (2:18-28)

After contrasting love for the world and love for God, John turns to a longer treatment of the contrast between truth and error. The apostle's encouragement that genuine believers *know and believe* the truth can be summarized in three points.

A. The Reason: Because of the Anointing from the Holy One (v. 20, 21, 27).

But you (v. 20) —

genuine believers are set in contrast to the heretical deserters of verses 18-19. Verse 27 basically says the same thing in contrast to the deceivers of verse 26.

have —

this is an *ongoing* possession grammatically.

anointing (v. 20, 27) —

verse 27 makes it clear that the anointing is a Teacher. See also Luke 4:14-18; Acts 10:38; 2 Cor. 1:21-22; John 14:26; 15:26-27; 16:13-14 (The references in the Gospel of John are promises to the apostles, who were channels of divine revelation. Those promises are, in fact, a guarantee of an inspired New Testament. The work of the Holy Spirit is obviously and applicably one of Teacher, however. These references in conjunction with the rest of Scripture mark out the "anointing" of 1 John to be the Divine Person of the Holy Spirit.)

from the Holy One (v. 20)/Him (v.27) —

Scripture attributes the title "Holy One" to both God (throughout Isaiah) and Jesus Christ (Mark 1:24; John 6:69; Acts 2:27). In John 16:7 the Spirit is sent by both the Father and the Son. The context of 1 John 2:18-28 seems to point to Christ as the sender, but the Apostle John seems to use personal pronouns which could refer grammatically and theologically to either Christ or God the Father, indicating that he saw no real need to clarify between the two *in these particular situations*. It is clear, however, that all true Christians have a resident truth teacher dwelling inside of them. He is from God, and in fact, God Himself.

And you all know (v. 20)/Teaches you about all things (v. 27) —

because of the context, these terms are most likely implicit references to the false teachers and their teachings (which most likely involved the "secret/higher knowledge"). John is saying, "No, the Holy Spirit has taught you the truth." The Word of God and the gospel does not change (cf. v. 24). In saying this, however, John is not denying the role of teachers in Christianity. In this very letter, John is taking the role of a teacher (cf. Eph. 4:11). The false teachers were denying Jesus as the Divine Christ of God (v. 22-23; cf. John 16:13-15—the true teacher teaches Christ and glorifies Christ).

B. The Results

1. We Remain in the Fellowship of Believers (v. 18-19)

Children —

John reminds his readers that they are under his spiritual oversight. This could also be especially applicable to the less mature believers who may be open to some of the heretical influences of those who had left the believing community.

the last hour —

the grammar does not suggest identity of the last hour as much as the quality or type of time that it now is. It is by character the last hour. Though John wrote 1900 years ago, it is still the last hour. We don't know the day or the hour of Christ's return (Matt. 24), but now as in John's day, the signs of nearing the end of the world and Christ's return are present.

antichrists —

those *against Christ*, as the compound word suggests. The false teachers in verse 19 are characterized by apostasy. They leave, and in doing so they manifest their true character as unbelievers. They claimed to be Christians, but they left the fellowship. If they had been genuine believers, "they would have remained with us" (that is in the fellowship of true believers who follow the Spirit-inspired, apostolic doctrine).

True Christians know and believe the truth, therefore they remain in the fellowship of true believers.

2. We Confess Christ (v. 22-23)

Who is the liar —

"The Greek text carries the article before the noun (liar) and should be translated 'the liar,' thus pointing up the unique character of this deceiver. His is the lie that exceeds all other lies in its awful significance, for his denial strikes at the very heart of the gospel. To deny the incarnation is to deny the validity of Christian truth altogether. If Jesus were not the God-man, at the same time fully God and fully man, He could not be the Savior. He must be fully man to die for man, and He must be fully God for His death to be of sufficient value to atone for sin" (Burdick, p. 200) (Cf. 4:2-3, 15; 2 John 7-9; Matt. 11:27.)

denies —

present tense. This is an ongoing practice. This is rejection of what the Bible claims about Jesus.

Whoever denies the Son does not have the Father —

the ramifications of this phrase are staggering. Every major cult and false religion in some way distorts the Person and/or work of Jesus Christ. Religions that claim to worship the one true God, but deny Jesus Christ as the Divine Son, do not in fact worship the true God.

confesses —

again the grammar points to an ongoing practice. To confess the Son is to agree with God and His Word about who Jesus is and what He did.

Because true Christians are taught by the Holy Spirit through the Word of God, they believe the truth. Therefore, they confess Jesus Christ, the Son of God, to be Savior and Lord (Rom. 10:9-10). He is from God to them—wisdom, righteousness, redemption and sanctification (1 Cor. 1:30).

3. We Abide/Remain in the True (Original) Gospel (v. 24)

As for you —

again the contrast with those who deny Christ.

abide —

remain/continue/dwell. Let the gospel of Christ dwell in you. This word carries the idea of being "at home" in you (Burdick, p. 203). In other words, continue believing and living out the truth which already lives in you.

from the beginning —

> this is a reference to their conversion, when they first heard and understood the gospel in a saving way.

> "If you keep true to the gospel of Christ, it will keep you true" (Reference unknown).

4. We Have the Promise of Eternal Life (v. 25)

this —

> refers to what immediately follows in the sentence—eternal life.

promise —

> God's promises never fail. (See under "eternal life." Also cf. 1 Thess. 5:24.)

eternal life —

> both duration and quality of life here and now (cf. John 3:15-16; 4:13-14; 5:24; 6:40, 47; 8:31-36; 10:28; 17:2-3).

5. We Need Not Be Deceived (v. 26-27)

These things —

> refer most naturally to verses 18-25.

those who are trying to deceive you —

> there were false teachers actively trying to "lead astray" these true believers, some sincerely and others with conscious deception.

> Christians have the Holy Spirit and the Word of God. We need never be deceived by false teaching.

C. The Responsibility of Believing the Truth (v. 28).

And now little children —

> John sums up his line of reasoning and applies the truth practically to his beloved spiritual children.

Abide in Him —

John repeats the command to abide in Christ. (Cf. v. 27 "you abide in Him" can be translated as a command, i.e., "abide in Him." In v. 27 John is affirming the teaching which the Holy Spirit originally taught them. Here in v. 28 the apostle commands them to abide for a slightly different purpose. It is abiding in Him for the purpose [so that] of being ready for Christ's appearing.)

appears —

points to the suddenness of Christ's coming, and it will be an event, not a process (Burdick, p. 208).

we may have —

John includes himself with all true believers in this responsibility.

confidence —

in Greek politics, this term meant "freedom of speech" (Burdick, p. 208).

shrink away from Him —

speaks of the shame on the day of Christ's return, of knowing the truth but not living it out. It could refer to a merely professing Christian who is not genuine, in the day of judgment. Or it may refer to a true believer who is ashamed of his lack of faithfulness at the "*Bema seat*" judgment (2 Cor. 5:10). In the context of the book as a whole, the first view seems to fit the best.

His coming —

Christ's royal presence/coming.

John 10:28 is from God's perspective; 1 John 2:28 is our responsibility.

Section Three

True Christians
Possessors of Eternal Life
Have Fellowship with
the God Who is Righteous

God is Righteous
1st John 2:29-4:6

Chapter 14
Practicing Righteousness

● ● ● ● ● ●

1 John 2:29

29) If you know that He is righteous, you know that everyone also who practices righteousness is born of Him.

> I. **True Christians (Possessors of Eternal Life) Practice Righteousness (2:29)**
>
>   A. Because of Our Righteous God(v. 29)
>   B. Because of Our New Birth (v. 29)

I. True Christians (Possessors of Eternal Life) Practice Righteousness (2:29)

A. Because of Our Righteous God

If you know —

This is not a statement of doubt, but a statement of argument (Gooding, p. 216). The apostle appeals to common sense—the genuine believer's righteous practice stems from the righteous character of God. John is building a logical argument of "if – then." It's almost as if he is saying, "If you know ('intuitively, for a fact' is the thrust of the word) that He is righteous (and you should), then you should conclude that everyone who practices genuine righteousness is born of Him."

He —

In v. 28, "He" obviously refers to Christ (cf. 1 John 2:1, which refers to Jesus Christ, the Righteous). But here in verse 29 the pronoun in the last half of the verse says that those who practice righteousness are "born of Him." Nowhere else in Scripture is anyone said to be born of Jesus (cf. John 3:6 - Spirit; 1 Pet.

1:23 - Word; but never Jesus). The context favors God the Father as the referent of both pronouns in verse 29 (cf. 3:1, 9; 4:7; 5:1, 4). It is clear, though, from all of John's writings that ". . . when John thinks of God in relation to men, he never thinks of Him apart from Christ. And he never thinks of Christ in His human nature without adding the thought of His divine nature." (Wescott, p. 83; quoted in Hiebert, p. 131).

righteous —

that which is completely right/just. What does the Bible mean when it says that God is righteous?

- perfection in everything - Dueteronomy 32:3-4
- God's ways are righteous - Hosea 14:9
- God's Word is righteous - Psalm 19:7-8
- God's judgment is righteous. What He does and decides is eternally just/correct/right - Psalm 9:7-8
- God is righteous in salvation - Isaiah 45:21
- God is righteous in forgiving sin - 1 John 1:9

God is utterly and irrefutably perfect, pure, just and right in all that He is, does, says, thinks, judges, commands and requires. He Himself is the standard of right, and He never contradicts Himself, His standards, or His character. He is reliable and faithful to always be just and do rightly.

know —

there are two different Greek words translated "know" here in verse 29. The first one means knowledge known intuitively as fact. The second one means a deduced or logically concluded knowledge. The thought is something like this: "If you know intuitively that He is righteous, you should have logically concluded and known by deduction that everyone who practices righteousness (as God defines it) is born of Him."

B. Because of the New Birth

everyone —

it is universally true that *whoever* practices true righteousness *as God defines it* (its standard and how to obtain it) has been born of God.

practices —

literally, "doing" righteousness. The grammatical construction of this word indicates a habit of doing righteousness. It does not mean uninterrupted righteousness or perfection. It does mean the direction of your life is characterized by righteousness.

righteousness —

refers to the particular righteousness mentioned above, the righteousness of God.

To live in righteousness is to avoid practicing sin, but not only that, it is to actively pursue what God says is right (in His Word) in both attitude and action. How can this be done in light of what God says about us (cf. Rom. 3:10-12; Ps. 143:2; Gen. 6:5; 8:21; Ecc. 7:20)? The answer is found at the end of 1 John 2:29— ". . . is born of Him." (Note the initial steps of practicing righteousness as seen in Luke 18:10-14 and Matt. 5:1-11—conviction of your own lack of righteousness and a plea for God's mercy and provision; see also 1 John 1:7-10).

is born of Him —

The verb is literally "has been born" of Him. "Of" speaks of the source of this birth. It means that the one who is habitually practicing righteousness *has already been born of God* and stands in that state of having been born of God. Only those already born of God can and do practice righteousness in His eyes (cf. 3:4-10). Notice verse 29 does not say that *if* you practice righteousness you *will be born* of God. No man can make himself righteous before God (Isa. 64:6). Only those born of God can live out true righteousness (cf. John 1:12-13; 3:1ff; 14:6; 1 John 5:1-5, 10-13; Acts 4:12; Gal. 2:16; Rom. 3:20-26; Isa. 45:21ff). True Christians will reflect the character of God—and *He is righteous.*

Don't forget the practical righteousness that justification produces (cf. Titus 2:11-14; 3:8; Eph. 2:10). How can we *do* righteousness practically (Ps. 119:1-3, 9-11, 33-40, 62-63, 75, 128, 137-140)? Psalm 119:176 sums it up—seek and love God's Word and cry to Him for help and mercy.

Him —

most likely God the Father (see above note under "He").

Chapter 15
Being Called a Son of God

● ● ● ● ● ●

1 John 3:1-3

1) See how great a love the Father has bestowed upon us, that we would be called children of God; and such we are. For this reason the world does not know us, because it did not know Him. 2) Beloved, now we are children of God, and it has not appeared as yet what we shall be. We know that when He appears, we shall be like Him, because we shall see Him just as He is. 3) And everyone who has this hope fixed on Him purifies himself, just as He is pure.

II.   Be Encouraged: True Christians (Possessors of Eternal Life) Have the Promised Hope of Ultimate Righteousness (3:1-3)

   A.   The Basis of Our Hope: The Father's Love (v. 1)
       1.   It Makes Us Children of God
       2.   It Makes Us Strangers to the World
   B.   The Future Consummation of Our Hope: Christ's Coming (v. 2)
   C.   The Present Result of Our Hope: Personal Purification (v. 3)

II. Be Encouraged: True Christians (Possessors of Eternal Life) Have the Promised Hope of Ultimate Righteousness (3:1-3)

Before the apostle elaborates on the issue of *doing* righteousness as a dominate characteristic of genuine believers, he reminds his readers of the promise/hope of ultimate righteousness (perfect Christ-likeness). It's as if John realizes afresh the incomprehensible and joyous wonder of what it means to be born of God. Amazing love and unending hope tie into his thoughts of God as righteous, and the believer as characterized by doing righteousness.

A. The Father's Love: the Basis of Our Hope (v. 1)

See —

a command to immediately look, behold and discern with the mind.

how great a love —

the root of "how great" originally conveyed the sense of "from what country" (Burdick, p. 229). This is love that is completely foreign to the human realm. John says, "Look—now!—at the amazing love of the Father who has caused us to be born again." This is incomprehensible love (cf. Rom. 5:8). The basis for our hope of perfect righteousness is grounded in the Father's love. This type of love in the Bible is a decision of the will to seek the highest good for the object of one's love. It is dependent on the lover's choice, not the receiver's worthiness.

The Father —

is none other than the Father of our Lord Jesus Christ through whom this amazing love is given. Because He is Christ's Father, He becomes the Father of all who are in Christ.

has bestowed —

God has not only demonstrated His love but, literally, "given" it us. It is a gift given in the past, with present, continuing results. God's love is also undeserved/unearned.

unto us —

John includes himself with all believers as a recipient of God's gracious gift of love. The most amazing part seems to be that God's love has been given to *us* (cf. Rom. 3 - sinners/enemies of His; Rom. 5:8-10).

1. It Makes Us God's children

called —

named or known as. This is how we are labeled by God.

children of God —

are those who share in the nature and inheritance of God, by His election and choice, and regenerative grace.

and such we are —

Not only are we *called* children of God, but by the decree and work of God the Holy Spirit—we *are*.

2. It Makes Us Unknown to the World

the world —

See also 1 John 2:15-17; 5:19. The people of the world are related to the world. We are related to God. To know someone is not just being aware of them, but having a relationship with them (i.e., personal contact and interaction). Because we are children of God, we can have *no spiritual relationship* with a non-Christian (except as a vessel of God's love for them).

did not know Him —

the context of verse 2 and the past tense of the verb both point to this pronoun as referring to Christ who came into history, yet was rejected by the world. Again, John shifts easily in his language between Christ and the Father, for they are One in essence (John 10:30). [Cf. John 1:10-13; 15:18-16:3, 33.] The world does not know—and did not know—God (Christ or the Father).

B. Christ's Coming: the Future Realization of Our Hope (v. 2)

Christ's appearing is the substance and future realization of our hope, which stems from God's love toward His own.

Beloved —

again the tender reference to those who are loved by both John and God.

now —

those who have trusted Christ are currently children of God. There is no process, system or catechism to ready oneself to be a child of God (cf. 5:1).

it has not appeared as yet what we shall be —

"We do not yet have detailed knowledge of our future state" (Burdick, p. 257). The glory of our future state is sure, but unimaginable (cf. Rom.8).

We know that, when He appears —

it is certain that when Christ is displayed openly (Hiebert, p. 137) we shall be like Him. The look at Christ directly will transform us forever. The more clearly we see Him now, through His Word, the more we are like Him now.

we shall be like Him —

See 2 Corinthians 3:18. We shall be perfectly Holy because He is perfectly Holy. We will have transformed, incorruptible bodies just like Him—immortality, purity, perfection and absolute righteousness (Rom. 8:18-30; Ps. 17:15; Eph. 1:4; 1 Cor. 15:47-57). This does not mean we will become little gods. We will be *like* Him, not equal to, or with Him (note God's supremecy in Rev. 21-22).

He is the Creator. We are creatures. We will be similar to Him reflecting His holiness and having resurrected bodies (cf. Burdick, p. 234).

because we will see Him just as He is —

See 1 Corinthians 13:12. To see God just as He is, we must be made like Him. Seeing Him will be both the reason for our transformation and the proof of our transformation.

> The whole person—body and soul—will be made completely flawless... We can't envision it now— "it doth not yet appear" —but we will finally be wholly and completely Christlike. This is the very purpose for which God called us in eternity past: "to be conformed to the image of His Son" (Rom. 8:29)... And when we see Christ, we will instantly and summarily be made utterly perfect, for we shall see Him as He is. Heaven is a perfect place for people made perfect. Perfection is the goal of God's sanctifying work in us. He's not merely making us better than we are; He is conforming us to the image of His Son. As much as glorified humanity can resemble incarnate, exalted deity, we will resemble our Lord. . . the utter perfection of heaven is the consummation of our salvation. (MacArthur, The Glory of Heaven, p. 118).

C. Personal Purification: the Present Result of Our Hope (v. 3)

everyone who has this hope —

without exception, everyone possessing this hope. "This hope" refers to the assurance of Christlikeness and seeing Christ as He is. Biblically, hope is not a wish or wishful thinking. Hope is a confident expectation that is based on the Word of God (Heb. 10:23), uncertain only as to time of consumation.

fixed on Him —

Jesus Christ and His return is the focal point.

purifies himself —

this is the human response to God's love and the hope to come (remember that God has already done, and is doing, the purifying as well; 1 John 1:7). The grammar suggests that those who possess this hope *habitually* seek the purification of their lives morally and spiritually (cf. Phil 3:10-14).

just as He is pure —

Jesus' purity/sinlessness/unspottedness is the standard. Jesus is pure, perfect, undefiled and obedient to His Father in everything.

Chapter 16
Not Practicing Sin
● ● ● ● ● ●

1 John 3:4-10a

4) Everyone who practices sin also practices lawlessness; and sin is lawlessness. 5) You know that He appeared in order to take away sins; and in Him there is no sin. 6) No one who abides in Him sins; no one who sins has seen Him or knows Him. 7) Little children, let no one deceive you; 8) the one who practices righteousness is righteous, just as He is righteous; the one who practices sin is of the devil; for the devil has sinned from the beginning. The Son of God appeared for this purpose, that He might destroy the works of the devil. 9) No one who is born of God practices sin, because His seed abides in him; and he cannot sin, because he is born of God. 10) By this the children of God and the children of the devil are obvious:

III. True Christians (Possessors of Eternal Life) Do Not Practice Sin (3:4-10a)

    A.   The Reasons (v. 4-9)
        1.   Because of What Sin is (v. 4)
        2.   Because of What Christ Came To Do and Did (v. 5a, 8b)
        3.   Because of Who Christ is (v. 5b, 7)
        4.   Because of Our Relationship with Christ (v. 6)
        5.   Because of Our New Birth (v. 8a, 9)
    B.   The Result: Our Practice Makes It Obvious Who We Belong To (v. 10)

III. True Christians (Possessors of Eternal Life) Do Not Practice Sin (3:4-10a)

Having concluded his detour of extolling the love of God, John moves back to the mainline of his argument by the thought-bridge of purity and righteousness (notice the connection and contrast between 2:29 and 3:4). Matthew 7:21-23 makes for an excellent illustration of the principle which lies behind this text in 1 John.

A. The Reasons

practices —

literally, "is doing." This is a consistent pattern of life for the individual who is included in "everyone" of verse 4.

sin —

"is a deliberate deviation from and infraction of the standard of right, a willful rebellion, arising from the deliberate choice of the sinner" (Hiebert, p. 141).

1. Because of What Sin is (v. 4)

Sin is lawlessness —

this isn't so much a transgression of a particular law or commandment, as it is an attitude of revolt or rebellion against God's supreme authority—and the authority of His Word (cf. Ps. 19:7-9). True Christians do not practice sin because of what it is—iniquity/rebellion/lawlessness against the authority of the God they claim to love.

Notice the contrast between verses 3 and 4. Everyone—without exception—who practices sin also practices lawlessness (v. 4). Everyone—without exception—who possesses the hope of Christ's return purifies himself (v. 3).

2. Because of What Christ Came to Do and Did (v. 5a, 8b)

And you know —

this is basic knowledge to all Christians. Christ came to take away sins. Christians have the anointing (2:20-21) of the Holy Spirit and know the truth.

He appeared —

Christ was manifested, not created. Nor did He come into being. He always existed, but at His incarnation, He *became visible*. True Christians don't practice sin because it is a fundamental truth of Christianity that Christ came to take away sins (cf. John 1:29).

in order to take away sins —

Pre-existent, eternal God became a man. And though He was sinless, He was crucified and rose again to take away His rebellious creatures' sins—not just the guilt and punishment, but the actual acts of sin themselves.

The Son of God (v. 8b) —

clear indication of the deity of Jesus Christ.

appeared for this purpose (v. 8b) —

the purpose of the incarnation of the Son of God (see also Hebrews 2).

that He might destroy the works of the devil (v. 8b) —

"destroy" means to render inoperative or powerless (Hiebert, p. 147). Christ came to break the controlling power of the devil who has been and still is in the business of sinning, killing and destroying—and inciting men to rebel against God (cf. Heb. 2:14). Revelation 20:11-15 tells of the final outcome.

3. Because of Who Christ is (v. 5b, 7)

and in Him there is no sin —

There is (present tense) no sin in Him. Jesus Christ is alive and without sin this very day as the resurrected God-Man in Heaven. Jesus has no sin nature, and no individual acts of sin can be attributed to Him. He is pure (cf. 3:3).

let no one deceive you (v. 7) —

it is quite possible that John's readers were being influenced by false teachers proclaiming some form of antinomian (literally, "without law") heresy (you can be right with God, yet live like the devil).

just as He is righteous (v. 7) —

Not only is Jesus Christ completely without sin, but He is our perfectly righteous standard and example. The One we worship, look to, love, and want to be like is righteous and right in all that He is and does. Christ is both our Savior and Model.

4. Because of Our Relationship with Christ (v. 6)

No one —

means exactly what it says—no one.

abides —

continual dwelling or remaining. This is *relationship* language.

in Him —

meaning Christ. Theologically this is a relationship with God in Christ Jesus.

sins —

present tense verb. It could be translated, "No one who is abiding in Him is (continually, or habitually) sinning, no one who is (habitually) sinning has seen Him or knows Him." Yet all Christians wrestle with patterns of seemingly habitual sin (cf. Rom. 7). What then is John saying in verse 6? The key is the context (particularly v. 8). The one who practices sin is "of the devil." Being "of the devil" characterizes this type of sin as indicative of a lost person. It is the type of sin which is similar to, or in imitation of the Satan's sin. Notice the nature of the devil's sin in verse 8. The NASB translated it "has sinned," but it is actually present tense—"is sinning from the beginning." Ever since his fall, Satan has had an unbroken, unbridled passion for sinning and a disregard for God's righteousness and Word. So applying this sense and context to verse 6, "the one who is sinning (from the very beginning of his birth in sin, he has lived and continues to live in a pattern of unrepentant, habitual rebellion and disregard for God's Word and authority as the dominant characteristic of his life) has not seen Him or known Him." Yes, it is habitual sin, but not the kind that genuine believers might battle with like Paul desribes in Romans 7. It is unrepentant sin and rebellion against the One who is Lord. Thus, if someone says he is a Christian, but his life doesn't show it by a tenderness and responsiveness to the Word of God and he keeps on sinning—that person in reality has not seen Christ or knows Christ. He is a liar.

has seen Him —

Christians have a relationship with Christ that stems from having seen Him by faith (cf. Heb. 11:24-27).

and knows Him —

this is personal, intimate, experiential knowledge of Christ. Note again the language of *relationship*.

5. Because of Who We Are Born of (v. 8a, 9)

of the devil —

> speaks of source of being, or origin. A genuine Christian is not "of the devil."

No one (v. 9) —

> without exception, no one who is born of God practices sin as a pattern of life.

> Notice John does not claim that Christians do not *commit* acts of sin, but only that they do not *practice* sin (cf. 1:8-10; 2:1).

because His seed abides in him (v. 9) —

> His seed is the new life that is given by the Holy Spirit, through the Word of God (cf. John 3:5-8; James 1:18; 1 Pet. 1:23-25).

he cannot sin (v. 9) —

> It is impossible for a genuine believer to sin as the continual/unbroken pattern of his life.

because he is born of God (v. 9) —

> this phrase tells why the regenerate man cannot sin as his way of life. In a nutshell, this is the argument of 1 John. The apostle is saying, since a genuine Christian has fellowship (participation/partaking) with the God who is light (truth and holiness), righteous, love and life—he therefore manifests light, righteousness, love and life.

B. The Result—Our Practice Makes Obvious Who We Belong to (v. 10)

By this —

> refers to the following summation in verse 10 of all that was said in verses 4-9.

children of God —

> true Christians. This term is reserved for those who have been born of God through faith in Jesus Christ.

children of the devil –

> cf. John 8:44ff.

are obvious —

> made manifest, visible; clearly seen.

Chapter 17
Loving One Another
• • • • • •

1 John 3:10b-24

10b) anyone who does not practice righteousness is not of God, nor the one who does not love his brother. 11) For this is the message which you have heard from the beginning, that we should love one another; 12) not as Cain, who was of the evil one and slew his brother. And for what reason did he slay him? Because his deeds were evil, and his brother's were righteous. 13) Do not marvel, brethren, if the world hates you. 14) We know that we have passed out of death into life, because we love the brethren. He who does not love abides in death. 15) Everyone who hates his brother is a murderer; and you know that no murderer has eternal life abiding in him. 16) We know love by this, that He laid down His life for us; and we ought to lay down our lives for the brethren. 17) But whoever has the world's goods, and beholds his brother in need and closes his heart against him, how does the love of God abide in him? 18) Little children, let us not love with word or with tongue, but in deed and truth. 19) We shall know by this that we are of the truth, and shall assure our heart before Him 20) in whatever our heart condemns us; for God is greater than our heart and knows all things. 21) Beloved, if our heart does not condemn us, we have confidence before God; 22) and whatever we ask we receive from Him, because we keep His commandments and do the things that are pleasing in His sight. 23) This is His commandment, that we believe in the name of His Son Jesus Christ, and love one another, just as He commanded us. 24) The one who keeps His commandments abides in Him, and He in him. We know by this that He abides in us, by the Spirit whom He has given us.

IV. True Christians (Possessors of Eternal Life) Show Themselves True by Their Love for the Brethren (3:10b-24)

A. It is a Love that Obeys God (v. 10b-12)

B. It is a Love that is Foreign to This World (v. 13-15)

C. It is a Love that Sacrifices for Others (v. 16-17)

D. It is a Love that Shows in the Sincerity of Our Lives (v. 18)

E. It is a Love that Brings Assurance (v. 19-24)

1. Assurance that We Are of the Truth (v. 19-20)

2. Assurance of Confident Access to God (v. 23-24)

3. Assurance of Intimate Union with God (v. 23-24)

IV. True Christians (Possessors of Eternal Life) Show Themselves True By Their Love for the Brethren (3:10b-24)

In the apostle's mind there is an undeniable connection between righteousness and love.

Here are five characteristics of genuine Christians' love.

A. It is a Love that Obeys God (v. 10b-12a)

nor —

connects the previous thought to the issue of love for the brethren.

love —

see also previous notes. This is present-tense love—love as a pattern of life.

his brother —

other professing Christians. Elsewhere in Scripture (Luke 10:27-37), God commands us to love our neighbor (meaning everybody), but John is evidently addressing a specific issue here. Maybe some of the deceivers (2:26) had no love for the Christian brotherhood.

for —

tells the reason as to why righteousness and love make obvious the origin of the professing person.

this is the message which you have heard from the beginning —

"the message" is the gospel. "The beginning" refers to when they were first converted to Christ. From the very outset, the gospel included the issues of love and righteousness. God's message—His Word—His gospel is one of faith, holiness, righteousness and love. A lack of love for others who are born of God is a sign of disobedience to God and even a lack of relationship with God. This love crosses all ethnic and political boundaries.

not as Cain —

John uses a negative example in verse 11, that is positively affirming verse 10 (cf. Gen. 4:1-16). Cain's deeds were evil because he was disobedient to God, which led to a lack of love and eventually to murder.

of the evil one —

See John 8:44.

slew —

> to butcher or slaughter.

B. It is a Love that is Foreign to this World (v. 13-15)

Do not marvel —

> stop being amazed that the world is perpetually hating you.

brethren —

> John here identifies with his readers. He too is a brother and subject to the hatred of the world.

if —

> "After words denoting wonder it is best translated *that*; as in Mk. 15:44, 'Pilate marvelled *that* he was already dead...'" (*A Manual Grammar of the Greek New Testament*, H.E. Dana and Julius R. Mantey, p. 246). The hatred is not uncertain, but *when* the hatred will be revealed is the issue of uncertainty.

the world —

> cf. 2:15ff. Does the world recognize you as one of its own, or as an enemy to its sinful agenda?

We know —

> intuitive knowledge known as fact.

we have passed out of death into life —

> we have migrated, or taken steps out of *death* (the realm of sin and separation from God), into life (the realm of God's life, intimacy with God and righteousness). See also John 5:24.

Because we love the brethren —

> we know we have passed from death to life *because* of the fruit of our lives. We love other Christians. This again is love as a way/pattern of life. Love for other believers is not just an added blessing, but an essential proof of reality.

Everyone —

> without exception.

hates —

> present tense way of life.

his brother —

> the Christian community and the individuals that make it up.

murderer —

> cf. Matt. 5:21-22.

and you know —

> is certain/automatic knowledge. Only forgiveness through faith in Christ can give a murderer eternal life (i.e., the Apostle Paul).

C.   It is a Love that Sacrifices for Others (v. 16-17)

We know —

> speaks of a lesson learned in the past by observation and reflection, with continuing results.

by this —

> points forward to the rest of verse 16.

He —

> literally "that One," referring to Christ.

laid down His life for us —

> Jesus laid aside His life as a garment for us. His love is seen in the fact that Christ—God in human flesh—laid down His life for us.

we ought —

> "we" is stressed in the original grammar. We are morally obligated/constrained/compelled as Christians to lay down our lives for the brethren (cf. John 13:35; Rom. 16:3-4).

But —

> in contrast to sacrificial loving and dying to self.

the world's goods —

> the life or livelihood to live in this world (world here is not used in its strictly evil sense).

beholds —

> not merely glancing casually, but taking a long look. "To appreciate and understand the circumstances of the case" (Brooke, p. 97 quoted from Thomas, p. 300). The term is present tense, meaning ongoing observation.

in need —

> literally, "having need."

and closes his heart against him —

> puts up a wall around his heart/bowels of compassion.

how does the love of God abide in him —

> a question that really doesn't need an answer.

D. It is a Love that Shows in the Sincerity of Our Lives (v. 18)

In many ways, verse 18 is a summary of verses 10-17.

Let us —

> John includes himself with his readers.

word or tongue —

> "From the repetition of [word] and [tongue] it would appear that the most prevalent deviation from genuine love was that of mere talk rather than loving action" (Burdick, p. 270).

but —

> strongly contrast mere talk with actions and sincerity as a loving way of life.

and truth —

> truth is added here to negate mere outward deeds that lack true love from the heart.

E. It is a Love that Brings Assurance (v. 19-24)

1. Assurance that We Are of the Truth (v. 19-20)

We shall know by this —

> refers back to verse 18—the sincere life that lives our love in deed and truth.

of the truth —

> who and what we derive our existence from is the truth, if verse 18 is true of us.

assure our heart before Him/in whatever our heart condemns us —

> As John has been telling us that true Christians are characterized by an obedient, sacrificial, sincere love, now he sees the need to give us some reassurance. It is in this area of love that many an honest Christian seems to feel his or her inadequacy the most. John even includes himself (*we* shall know/*our* heart). As we see ourselves fall short so often in thought and deed, we have the objective facts to look at. We do seek and have lived out love to some extent in

deed and truth. And verse 20 gives an even greater comfort— "God is greater than our heart, and knows all things." We have faith in God alone Who is our hope. He knows us better than we know ourselves. He never overlooks our sins. He hates sin. But he has taken care of our sin in Christ (1:7). He is our loving Father who is the very source of any love we do have (4:19). He understands, knows, hears and has given us our true heart's cry for love, holiness and obedience. He put it there. It is to God's perfect understanding that Peter appealed to as his heart was pricked concerning his own hypocrisy and lack of love (cf. John 21:17). So when doubts and fears assail you concerning who you belong to—go back and think of the test of love. Do you desire to obey God? Does the world separate from you because of your love? Do you sacrifice for other Christians? Do you live a sincere life of love? Yet you hear the doubts and see the failures. Be encouraged, God knows all. He is greater than even an over-sensitive conscience. Never quickly dismiss a guilty conscience, but always analyze your conviction *in light of the Scriptures.*

2. Assurance of Confident Access to God (v. 21-22)

if our heart does not condemn us —

a life of love that can be evaluated objectively quiets a sensitive heart. If our heart does not condemn us, we feel the freedom to approach God *on His terms.* See Hebrews 4:16.

confidence before God —

this is freedom of speech, as it were, directly before God. It is not that our life of love merits a hearing with God. It is however the objective test by which we can know that we do have the assurance of confident access to God.

whatever —

this term is qualified only by the logical restraints delineated in verse 22 (we keep His commandments — therefore we don't ask for anything outside His will; and we do the things that are pleasing in His sight — therefore we don't ask for things that aren't pleasing to Him).

we ask —

this is not just a one-time promise, but asking as a way of life.

keep/do —

present tense. Obedience is the pattern of life.

commandments/things that are pleasing in His sight —

> knowing and seeking to obey from the heart—God's will through His Word. Again, perfection is not commanded, but having the direction toward it is a must (cf. 1:8-2:1).

> Note some scriptural prerequisites for answered prayer — John 16:23-24; James 1:5-7; 4:2-3; Mark 11:25; Psalm 66:18; 1 John 5:14-15.

3. Assurance of Intimate Union with God (v. 23-24)

And this is His commandment —

> As John moves from the existence of an obedient and faithful life as a condition for assurance and answered prayer, He summarizes all of God's commandments into one (with two parts—faith in Christ and love for one another) all-encompassing commandment in verse 23. Verse 23 is like an explanatory parenthesis to what he has just said in verse 22, and is about to say in verse 24.

that we believe in the name of His Son Jesus Christ —

> "We" indicates the apostle's inclusion of himself under the authority of this command. "Believe" is particularly thematic in the Gospel of John. It carries the idea of faith in and entrustment to. "Name" stands for all that a person is and what he represents (cf. 3 John 7; Acts 3:16; Ps. 20:7). "Jesus" speaks of Christ's humanity. He is fully man. "Christ" speaks of Jesus as the Divine King. "His Son" speaks of Jesus as God. He is fully God. True Christianity is a call to faith in, and entrustment to, the God-Man, Jesus Christ—who He is and what He did (substitutionary death and victorious resurrection).

and love one another, just as He commanded us —

> this second part of the commandment is really just faith in action (cf. John 13:34-35; Gal. 5:6).

> In verse 24, the apostle links faith, love and obedience as the sources of Christian assurance. These are the three practical tests of genuine Christianity.

the one who keeps His commandments —

> present tense/habitual keeping.

abides in Him and He in him—

> Mutual dwelling and remaining in one another is the thought. This is intimate, relational language. (Cf. Isa. 40 for the greatness of this God who has chosen to be intimate with creatures such as us.)

And we know by this —

points backward to the objective tests of love, faith and obedience. But as the verse goes on to say, "it is by the Spirit whom He has given us" that these come to fruition.

the Spirit —

the Holy Spirit of God. He inspires us to confess Christ (4:1-6), and He empowers us to obedience and love (4:12-13).

Whom He has given us —

the gift of the Spirit is *not earned* by obedience. He is a *gift* given at the time of salvation, and He produces that faith-wrought love and obedience (cf. Gal. 5:22-23).

Chapter 18
Discerning Truth from Error

••••••

1 John 4:1-6

1) Beloved, do not believe every spirit, but test the spirits to see whether they are from God, because many false prophets have gone out into the world. 2) By this you know the Spirit of God: every spirit that confesses that Jesus Christ has come in the flesh is from God; 3) and every spirit that does not confess Jesus is not from God; this is the spirit of the antichrist, of which you have heard that it is coming, and now it is already in the world. 4) You are from God, little children, and have overcome them; because greater is He who is in you than he who is in the world. 5) They are from the world; therefore they speak as from the world, and the world listens to them. 6) We are from God; he who knows God listens to us; he who is not from God does not listen to us. By this we know the spirit of truth and the spirit of error.

    V. True Christians (Possessors of Eternal Life) Can and Must Discern Truth from Error(4:1-6)

        A.   The Warning/Command to Discern (v. 1)

        B.   The First Test: Christological (v. 2-3)

        C.   The Assurance of Victory (v. 4)

        D.   The Second Test: Bibliological (v. 5-6)

V. True Christians (Possessors of Eternal Life) Can and Must Discern Truth from Error (4:1-6)

The apostle, having just addressed assurance as ultimately coming from the Spirit of God, now calls his readers to discern between truth and error—the Spirit and the spirits.

A. The Warning/Command to Discern (v. 1)

Beloved —

John once again shows his love (as well as God's) and pastoral concern in this tender address.

do not believe every spirit —

a present-tense command to not trust, or give credence to every spirit (cf. Burdick, p. 292). The term "spirit" is further defined at the end of the verse by the phrase "many false prophets." What do false prophets do but proclaim a false message? "To believe the prophet [teacher] was to believe the spirit who spoke through him." (Burdick, p. 292).

but test the spirits —

in contrast to giving credence to every teacher who claims to be from God, keep on testing the veracity of the teachers who are teaching you (by their message; cf. 1 Thess. 5:19-22; Deut. 13:1-5). In the O. T. a test of a genuine prophet was what he said about God. John in verse 2 says that the test of a genuine prophet has to do with what He says about Jesus.

because many false prophets have gone out into the world —

the reason for this call to discernment.

B. The First Test: Christological (v. 2-3)

By this you know —

"By this" refers to what follows in verses 2-3. "Know" is knowledge obtained by observation.

the Spirit of God —

the message has been genuinely approved by the *Holy Spirit*. It is the Holy Spirit's ministry to testify to Christ and glorify Him as Lord (John 15:26; 16:13-15; 1 Cor. 12:3).

every spirit —

John is not claiming that there are many Holy Spirits (plural), but that the many teachers who do confess Christ—their spirits are under control of *the* Holy Spirit.

confesses —

to confess is to affirm (publicly) allegiance to and faith in the one you are confessing. It is agreeing with God about who Christ is (which is revealed only in the Bible). Again the Greek indicates an ongoing state of confession, not just a one time event.

Jesus Christ has come in the flesh —

this is a confession of faith in and allegiance to Jesus Christ—the Divine Son of God who is King—as having become incarnate in human flesh. Theologically, Christ's incarnation cannot be separated from His righteous/sinless life, sacrificial/substitutionary death on the cross, and resurrection from the grave.

Verse 3 is the restatement in negative terms of the same test. See also 2:18ff. The message is clear. Any message, teaching, teacher, prophet or prophecy that denies Jesus Christ as fully God and fully man—solely through faith in His Name may a person be made right with God—is not from God, but the antichrist.

C. The Assurance of Victory (v. 4)

You are from God, little children —

"you" is emphatic in the Greek. John wants to assure and comfort his "little children" that they stand in contrast to the antichrists of verse 3.

You have overcome them —

"them" refers to the false prophets with their demonically inspired messages. "Overcome" means to prevail, or be victorious—even to conquer. This is a past event with current results.

because greater is He who is in you than he who is in the world —

John here gives the reason for their victory. Specifically, John is talking about the Holy Spirit in the context of verses 2-3 (cf. 2:20-21, 27). First John 5:19 makes it clear that the "he who is in the world" is Satan. The key to knowing and discerning truth from error is having the Holy Spirit live in you.

D. The Second Test: Bibliological (v. 5-6)

They are from the world —

"They," in contrast to the true believers of verse 4, refers to the false teachers and their message, which is demonically inspired by deceiving spirits. "From" or "of" speaks of origin, while "world" again speaks of the evil world system opposed to God and His Word.

they speak as from the world —

their speech has its source in the system controlled by Satan (5:19).

and the world listens to them —

"listens" means to give credence to and obey.

We —

is emphatic in the Greek and in direct opposition to the "they" of verse 5. "They" are false prophets, but "we" are truly from God. Here, John is referring to the *apostolic witness* (and by implication, those who teach true apostolic doctrine as contained in the New Testament).

he who knows God -

speaking of a genuine believer/Christian.

listens to us —

speaks of believing obedience. This is a pattern of heeding New Testament truth. God's people listen to and obey God's Word (cf. John 8:31-37, 43-47; 10:4, 5, 8, 16, 26-27; 18:37). "Us" again referring to the apostolic witness.

he who is not from God —

not a true believer/Christian.

does not listen to us —

He who has his origin in the world won't listen to the truth of God's Word; it repels him.

By this we know the spirit of truth and the spirit of error —

"By this" refers to listening to God's Word, as seen earlier in the verse. In verse 2, "by this" refers to the confessing of Christ. The "we" is no longer emphatic, thus noting that John includes himself with the readers (and all true believers). He is no longer referring solely to the apostolic witness (see note above).

The tests of truth are clear:

- 1) What do they teach about Christ?
- 2) Do they (and those who listen to them) affirm and seek to obey the clear teaching of God's Word?

Section Four

True Christians

Possessors of Eternal Life

Have Fellowship with

the God Who is Love

God is Love

1st John 4:7-5:5

Chapter 19
Being Born to Love
• • • • • •

1 John 4:7-12

7) Beloved, let us love one another, for love is from God; and everyone who loves is born of God and knows God. 8) The one who does not love does not know God, for God is love. 9) By this the love of God was manifested in us, that God has sent His only begotten Son into the world so that we might live through Him. 10) In this is love, not that we loved God, but that He loved us and sent His Son to be the propitiation for our sins. 11) Beloved, if God so loved us, we also ought to love one another. 12) No one has beheld God at any time; if we love one another, God abides in us, and His love is perfected in us.

    I.   **True Christians (Possessors of Eternal Life) Are Compelled to Love (4:7-12)**

         A.   Because of Who God is (v. 7-8)

         B.   Because of What God Has Done in Christ (v. 9-11)

             1.   He Has Graciously Revealed Himself (v. 9)

             2.   He Has Mercifully Atoned for Sin (v. 10-11)

         C.   Because of What God is Doing in Us (v. 12)

I. True Christians (Possessors of Eternal Life) Are Compelled to Love (4:7-12)

After a short excursus dealing with discernment of spirits, truth and error, the apostle John moves back to the subject of love, which he had been dealing with at the end of chapter three. But this time he makes another monumental statement about the character of God, thus beginning the third major movement in the argumentation of 1 John. God is love (v. 7; cf. 1:5—God is light; 2:29—He is righteous), therefore genuine Christians walk in love (which is indivisible from a life of faith and obedience/righteousness).

Here we see three reasons true Christians are compelled to love.

A. Because of Who God is (v. 7-8)

Beloved —

four out of the six times John uses this familiar address, he is writing about the issue of love.

let us love —

could be translated as an exhortation to love (as here and in most Bible translations), but the form of the word can also be translated as a statement of fact— "*we love.*" "The main point being expressed in verses 7-16 is not an exhortation to love, but a declaration that Christians do love because they have been born of God, who is love. To translate the verb, 'let us love', would seem to suggest that by loving, one is somehow born of God and comes to know God. Actually the sequence is just the reverse. Those who are born of God and know God are therefore able to love." (Burdick, p. 317). A good translation would be— "Beloved, we are habitually loving one another because love is from God, and everyone who loves is born of God and knows God."

one another —

the specific objects of our love in this context are other Christians. In Matthew 5 we are to love our enemies, but here it is the community of believers in Christ. Evidently the false teachers were showing their true colors through a lack of love for the Christian brotherhood.

for love is from God —

this statement explicitly gives the reason that genuine believers love other Christians. God is the source and origin of self-giving love.

and everyone who loves is born of God —

the reason true Christians are compelled to love is because they are born of the God who is love (see 2 Pet. 1:4—born-again believers are partakers of the divine nature). God is the Father of all who love sacrificially.

and knows God —

this is again language that denotes a personal, intimate relationship.

The one who does not love does not know God —

the one who doesn't practice this self-giving love as a pattern of life does not— and has never—known God. There is no relationship. This person has never been born again.

for God is love —

the Greek is constructed in such a way that it can be translated basically only this way. You could not say, "love is God." God defines what love is. He is also holy, righteous, just, jealous and full of wrath against His enemies (Nahum 1). His love compels Him to be all these things. God's attributes exist in perfect harmony with one another—without contradiction. Notice the end of verse 7 and verse 8— "love" has no direct object. It is a genuine believer's mode of life, whatever the object.

B. Because of What God Has Done in Christ (v. 9-11)

1. He Revealed Himself

By this —

refers to what follows in verse 8.

the love of God —

God's love for His mankind (cf. John 3:16).

was manifested —

God's love was made known. It became unmistakably clear and visible at the time of the incarnation of Jesus Christ. God became a man and came to men. Notice it does not say that God's love started when He sent His Son. His love has always existed.

in us —

among us.

God has sent —

"sent" speaks of a special mission in the past with ongoing results. The One God commissioned and sent continues to have the authority of God.

His only begotten Son into the world —

"only begotten" refers to the unique status of Jesus (the only one of His kind— Son of God). Again, "His. . .Son" speaks of Christ as very God. The Creator came to His creation (the world).

so that we might live through Him —

"The statement implies that those to whom the Son was sent were spiritually dead (Eph. 2:1, 5), but He came to give them life." (Hiebert, p. 201). This is not just eternal life in the future, but eternal life is a present experience and reality (cf. John 3:36). Notice the Possessor and Mediator of this life— "through Him." Spiritual life is given only through Jesus Christ, the Son of God.

2. He Atoned for Sin

In this is love —

again refers to the rest of verse 10 which defines love in a very unique way.

Not that we loved God, but that He loved us —

"Love does not originate in man." (Burdick, p. 323). God takes the initiative in every love relationship between Himself and His creation.

and sent His Son to be the propitiation for our sins —

this was the mission that God sent His only begotten to accomplish. "Propitiation" speaks of the satisfaction of the wrath of a Holy God against sin (cf. note on 2:2). Christ became the only satisfactory sacrifice for sin. God's justice, mercy and love meet at the cross of Jesus Christ.

This is the very heart of the gospel. The "good news" is not that God is willing to overlook sin and forgive sinners. That would compromise God's holiness. That would leave justice unfulfilled. That would trample on true righteousness. Furthermore, that would not be love on God's part, but apathy.

The *real* good news is that God Himself, through the sacrifice of His Son, paid the price of sin. He took the initiative ("not that we loved God, but that He loved us"). He was not responding to anything in sinners that made them worthy of His grace. On the contrary, His love was altogether undeserved by sinful humanity. The sinners for whom Christ died were worthy of nothing but His wrath. As Paul wrote, "Christ died for the *ungodly*. For one will hardly die for a righteous man; though perhaps for the good man someone would dare even to die. But God demonstrates His own love toward us, in that *while we were yet sinners*, Christ died for us" (Rom. 5:7-8, emphasis added).

Because God is righteous, He must punish sin; He cannot simply absolve guilt and leave justice unsatisfied. But the death of Christ totally satisfied God's justice, His righteousness, and His holy hatred of sin.

Some people recoil at the thought of an innocent victim making atonement for guilty sinners. They like the idea that people should pay for their own sins. But take away this doctrine of substitutionary atonement and you have no gospel at all. If the death of Christ was anything less than a guilt offering for sinners, no one could ever be saved. But in Christ's death on the cross, there is the highest possible expression of divine love. He, who is love, sent His precious Son to die as an atonement for sin. If your sense of fair play is outraged by that— good! It ought to be shocking. It ought to be astonishing. It ought to stagger you. Think it through, and you'll begin to get a picture of the enormity of the price God paid to manifest His love (MacArthur, *The Love of God*, pp. 36-38).

Beloved, if God so loved us, we also ought to love one another —

As recipient of God's love (i.e., "beloved" and "so" or thus loved us), we are morally obligated (**ought**) to love those for whom Christ died, because we have become partakers of the divine life through Christ.

C. Because of What God is Doing in His People (v. 12)

No one has beheld God at any time —

no man has seen God in His full essence as Spirit (John 4:24). Yes, men have seen Christ who is the incarnate God-Man (John 1:18; 14:9). Yes, men have seen O. T. Theophanies (Isa. 6; Ex. 33:22). But no one has observed God in all His fullness (cf. 1 Tim. 1:17).

if we love one another, God abides in us —

"In some sense, loving one another must replace seeing God in His essential being. Although God cannot be seen in His essence, since He is love (v. 8), He can be seen directly in His people when they love one another." (Burdick, p. 325). God dwells in us through His Holy Spirit. Love is evidence that God abides/dwells in us, not the condition. Again, here "love" is a present tense verb denoting a pattern of life.

and His love is perfected in us —

God's love reaches its intended goal in us when we sacrificially love other believers (cf. John 13:34-35; 15:12-17; 1 John 3:16-17).

Chapter 20
Being United with God

• • • • • •

1 John 4:13-19

13) By this we know that we abide in Him and He in us, because He has given us of His Spirit. 14) And we have beheld and bear witness that the Father has sent the Son to be the Savior of the world. 15) Whoever confesses that Jesus is the Son of God, God abides in him, and he in God. 16) We have come to know and have believed the love which God has for us. God is love, and the one who abides in love abides in God, and God abides in him. 17) By this, love is perfected with us, that we may have confidence in the day of judgment; because as He is, so also are we in this world. 18) There is no fear in love; but perfect love casts out fear, because fear involves punishment, and the one who fears is not perfected in love. 19) We love, because He first loved us.

II. **Be Encouraged: True Christians (Possessors of Eternal Life) Can Have Assurance of a Personal Relationship with the God Who is Love [Mutual Indwelling] (4:13-19)**

    A. The Basis for Our Assurance (v. 13-16)

        1. The Holy Spirit (v. 13)

        2. Confirmed Faith in the Apostolic Testimony of Christ (v. 14-15)

        3. Active Love Which Stems from Faith in God (v. 16)

    B. The Benefits of Our Assurance (v. 17-18)

        1. Confidence in the Day of Judgment (v. 17)

        2. Freedom from Fear (v. 18)

    C. The Bottom Line about Love and Assurance (v. 19)

II. Be Encouraged: True Christians (Possessors of Eternal Life) Can Have Assurance of a Personal Relationship with the God who is Love (Mutual Indwelling) (4:13-19)

As John continues his discussion on love, he now unites two great tests to give believers a framework for affirming that God dwells in them, and they in Him. These two tests are faith in the truth and love in action. This section is much less of an exhortation than the previous two. It focuses more on the affirmation and assurance of the genuine Christian who most likely sees his failures in this area of love.

Here we see three truths vitally connected to our assurance of a personal relationship with the God who is love.

A. The Basis of Our Assurance (v. 13-16)

1. The Holy Spirit (v. 13)

By this we know —

> points forward to the rest of verse 13 (God's gift of the Holy Spirit). The term "know" speaks of a process of acquiring knowledge through experience, observation and instruction (Burdick, p. 327). We've learned and grown in our knowledge that we abide in God.

we abide in Him and He in us —

> "abide" again means to dwell or remain. "In Him" speaks of God (cf. v. 12). This is language denoting a personal relationship and mutual indwelling. These are terms of intimacy.

because He has given us of His Spirit —

> "We know" because God has given us His Spirit (cf. Rom. 8:15-16; Eph. 1:13-14; 1 Cor. 2:10-12). "Of His Spirit" literally means "out of His Spirit He has given to us." John 3:34 says Jesus was given the Spirit *without measure*. Here, the phrase simply means that God has given us His very own presence in the Person of His Spirit.

So the basis of Christian assurance of a relationship with God starts with the inner witness of the Holy Spirit. But it does not rest solely on a subjective understanding of God's presence "in our hearts." God uses the objective witness of the Bible—the apostolic witness (cf. v. 14-15).

2. Confirmed Faith in the Apostolic Testimony of Christ (v. 14-15)

And we have beheld and bear witness —

> The "we" is emphatic in the Greek. The nature of the verbs "beheld" and "bear witness" point also to the fact that "we" is a reference to the apostles and eyewitnesses (whose inspired record is now given to us in the New Testament). "Beheld" means a careful, studied, past contemplation and examination with present, ongoing results. "To bear witness" is to testify of something or someone (see Acts 5:29-32). The construction of the grammar is reminiscent of 1 John 1:1-2, or even John 1:14-15.

> The assurance of mutual indwelling with God comes from the Holy Spirit— through the objective witness of Scripture concerning Jesus Christ and His saving work (cf. John 15:26-27).

that the Father has sent the Son to be the Savior of the world —

> God the Father sent God the Son on a specific mission in the past (the incarnation) with continuing results. Christ is described as "Savior of the world." He is the only sufficient Savior the world (sinful, lost humanity) can ever have.

Whoever confesses that Jesus is the Son of God —

> Assurance of a personal relationship with God comes by the Holy Spirit, who uses the apostolic testimony now recorded in Scripture, to produce confession of faith in the Person and work of Jesus Christ, the Son of God. "Whoever" suggests that the only limitation on salvation is faith in Christ.

abides in him, and he in God —

> cf. above. Again, language denoting mutual indwelling and intimate fellowship/relationship.

3. Active Love Which Stems from Faith in God (v. 16)

And we have come to know and have believed —

> Here the "we" is still emphatic, but the nature of the verbs and the context of verse 15 indicates that this statement includes all true Christians, and is not limited to the apostles and eyewitnesses. John says that knowledge and faith (belief) go hand in hand spiritually. You can't have true faith without knowledge of the truth. And you can't have true knowledge of God without faith (cf. John 6:69) —and both are gracious gifts of God.

the love which God has for us —

Literally, "in us." God's love is not just a love for us, but a love that possesses and lives in us and flows through us to others (cf. John 17:25-26).

God is love —

John goes back to the foundation of it all. In His character, God defines love and is self-giving for the ultimate good of those He loves.

and the one who abides in love abides in God, and God abides in him —

Those who habitually dwell in love give proof that they are habitually dwelling in God, and God is habitually abiding in them. Our living in love does not *make* God abide in us. It merely proves (or makes visible) that He *does* live in us.

The basis of our assurance that we have a relationship with God stems from the Holy Spirit in our hearts, who uses God's Word concerning Christ as Savior, to lead us to confess Him as the Son of God—in turn, then, we are compelled by faith to live out the love of God in us. Assurance comes through Spirit-wrought faith in Jesus as Savior, which leads to a life of sacrificial love.

B. The Benefits of Our Assurance (v. 17-18)

1. Confidence in the Day of Judgment (v. 17)

By this —

refers to what John has just said at the end of v. 16. In other words, "by God's indwelling and thus your living out sacrificial love, God's love reaches its intended purpose or goal—perfection."

with us —

carries the idea of our cooperation and participation with God in this process of love's completion.

that we may have confidence —

boldness or openness toward God.

in the day of judgment —

cf. 1 John 2:28; John 5:22-24. In the day when God judges all who have not received Christ, believers will have confidence because of their faith in Christ, stemming solely from the grace of God, which has enabled them to live a life of love.

because as He is so also are we in this world —

> "He" is literally, "that One." Note that John says that as Christ *is*—not was, but is—so are we in this world. Believers are *in Christ*—accepted in the Beloved, Ephesians says. Just as Christ is the embodiment of the invisible God who is love, believers are in a sense representatives of the God who is love—to a lost and dying world.

2. Freedom from Fear (v. 18)

fear —

> in this context "fear" is contrasted with "confidence" and "love" (v. 17). This is not godly fear and reverence. This is fear of punishment and torment. "Here fear has to do with condemnation; love has to do with assurance of salvation... Fear is self-centered. Love is other's centered." (Burdick, p. 336).

but perfect love casts out fear —

> "but" introduces a contrast to fear. "Perfect love" does not mean flawless, uninterrupted love. But it is love that comes to maturity as it is lived out in the general direction of a Spirit-filled life. Living out love by faith in Christ as Savior and Lord *casts out* fear of judgment.

because fear involves punishment —

> innate to this type of fear is an ongoing punishment that exists in the here and now, not just future retribution.

the one who fears is not perfected in love —

> fear of punishment-driven "love" (if you can call it that) is not God's intended goal and gives no true assurance of a relationship with God. True Christians should not be compelled to love and obedience because they fear punishment. In fact freedom from fear should mark their lives as different. But their love and obedience should be an outflow in response to God's first loving them, even though they were—and are—so completely unworthy of His love (cf. 2 Cor. 5:14).

C. The Bottom Line About Love and Assurance (v. 19)

We love, because He first loved us —

> Christian assurance should rest in the fact that it is God who is the ultimate source of faith and love in their lives. He gets all the credit, glory and praise for any sacrificial love we possess and live out.

Chapter 21
Overcoming the World
• • • • • •

1 John 4:20-5:5

20) If someone says, "I love God," and hates his brother, he is a liar; for the one who does not love his brother whom he has seen, cannot love God whom he has not seen. 21) And this commandment we have from Him, that the one who loves God should love his brother also. 1) Whoever believes that Jesus is the Christ is born of God, and whoever loves the Father loves the child born of Him. 2) By this we know that we love the children of God, when we love God and observe His commandments. 3) For this is the love of God, that we keep His commandments; and His commandments are not burdensome. 4) For whatever is born of God overcomes the world; and this is the victory that has overcome the world, our faith. 5) Who is the one who overcomes the world, but he who believes that Jesus is the Son of God?

III. True Christians (Possessors of Eternal Life) Cannot Separate Love, Faith and Obedience: They Overcome the World (4:20-5:5)

    A.   We Cannot Separate Love from Love (v. 20-21)

    B.   We Cannot Separate Faith and Love (v. 1)

    C.   We Cannot Separate Love and Obedience (v. 2-3a)

    D.   We Cannot Separate Obedience and Faith (v. 3b-5)

III. True Christians (Possessors of Eternal Life) Cannot Separate Love, Faith and Obedience: They Overcome the World (4:20-5:5)

John now begins to conclude the main portion of his argument by showing his readers that genuine Christianity is marked by faith in the Christ, obedience to God's Word, which is lived out in a life of love (especially toward other Christians).

A. We Cannot Separate Love from Love: Test #1 (v. 20-21)

You can't separate love for God from love for your brothers.

If someone says, "I love God" —

literally, "I am loving God" (a claim of ongoing love for God).

and hates his brother —

this is a life consistently showing hatred by a lack of sacrificial love for other confessing Christians.

he is a liar —

His character is false (cf. 1:6; 2:4, 22; John 8:44). "However loudly we may affirm ourselves to be Christians, our habitual sin, denial of Christ and selfish hatred expose us as the liars we are. Only holiness, faith and love can prove the truth of our claim to know, possess and love God" (Stott, p. 170).

for the one who does not love his brother whom he has seen, cannot love God whom he has not seen —

"It is easy to deceive oneself. The truth, however, is plain. Every claim to love God is a delusion if it is not accompanied by unselfish and practical love for our brethren" (Stott, p. 171). The veracity of our life in God is demonstrated by His freedom to love others through us.

and this commandment we have from Him … —

God, through the Lord Jesus Christ commands that there be no separation of love for God and love for other Christians (Matt. 22:36-40—neighbor is broad enough to include "brother"; John 13:34-35; 15:12).

B. We Cannot Separate Faith and Love: the New Birth (v. 1)

Faith in Christ brings new birth and love for the Father. Love for the Father cannot be separated from love for others who are born of Him.

Whoever believes that Jesus is the Christ —

anyone, without exception, who is continually believing the Bible's testimony as to who Jesus is. Belief in Christ implies submission to Him as Lord and Savior (Rom. 10:9-10; John 3:36; cf. Gal. 2:20; John 6:15-71).

is born of God —

has been born of God in the past with present, ongoing results. The one who has faith in Christ stands in the state of having been born of God (cf. John 3:3ff). He is truly alive.

and whoever loves the Father loves the child born of Him —

It is obvious who those are who have been born of God through faith in Christ—they love the Father. It is just as obvious that those who love the Father will love others who have been born of God.

C. We Cannot Separate Love and Obedience: Test #2 (v. 2-3a)

Love for God's children stems from love for God, which is inseparable from heart obedience to God.

By this we know that we love the children of God —

The next logical question after reading verse 1 is, "How then can I know that I'm loving the children of God?" John anticipates the question and answers it in verses 2-3. "By this" points forward to verses 2-3. By this we "know" by experience, that we *are loving* the children of God.

When we love God and observe His commandments —

"When" is used in verse 2 to convey the thought of simultaneous action. We are loving God's children not after, or if we love God and obey His commandments, but at the same time. "Observe" is literally "doing" (present tense).

Verse 3 more fully explains verse 2 and the relationship between love and obedience. John is explaining what true love is by equating it with obedience. Yet the end of verse 3 rules out any grudging obedience that is in reality void of love.

For this is the love of God —

i.e., love for God. How can a man love God (cf. v. 3)?

that we keep His commandments —

The word "keep" is different from "observe" in verse 2. Here the term carries with it the idea of an *internal and external* (but not merely outward) obedience. To put it very simply—walk with God in *heart obedience* as well as external conformity. Again the verb is present tense, giving the habitual or ongoing sense.

What are God's commandments? (Cf. Ps. 119:172; 2 Jn 9; Luke 11:28; John 17:17.) Love for God and obedience to the Bible are one and the same—not grudging, burdensome obedience, but faith-driven obedience, motivated from love.

D. We Cannot Separate Obedience and Faith: Victory (v. 3b-5)

Obedience that does not stem from genuine faith in Jesus Christ as Savior and Lord is not true obedience, and therefore not true love for God.

and His commandments are not burdensome —

"Burdensome" speaks of an oppressive load. Remember Jesus words in Matthew 11:30; John 14:15. Love lightens the load (cf. Gen. 29:20). The entire phrase again re-emphasizes the fact that true obedience is not grudging.

for—

gives the reason God's commandments (and keeping them for that matter) are not burdensome.

whatever —

emphasizes "not the man, but his birth from God which conquers." (Plummer, p. 112; quoted in Burdick, p. 346).

is born of God —

again the grammar points to being currently in the state of having been born of God. Christians are no longer dead in trespasses and sin. They now have the ability and love-driven desire to obey.

overcomes the world —

conquers, prevails over, and is victorious over the evil system hostile to God and His Word. The world wants to make God's Word (and obedience to it) a hardship and oppressive. But a true believer is born of God (v. 1), and whatever is born of God overcomes the world.

The battle is against worldly thinking. God's commandments are an unbearable burden to this world we live in. God's Word becomes a burden to us when we buy into the world's mindset. Worldly thinking tells us that it is *not* in our best interest and for our ultimate good that we obey God's Word. But the truth is that God wants only the very best for us.

and this is the victory that has overcome the world—our faith —

When a person comes to Christ at conversion (through faith), God gives him or her the power to gain victory over the world and its mindset. Faith (submissive trust in Christ) conquers worldly thinking.

And who is the one who overcomes the world, but he who believes that Jesus is the Son of God —

Confidence/faith/personal trust in Jesus as the God-Man of Scripture—and as your personal Savior—is the key to present, continuing victory/triumph over the world (and its "burdensome thinking"; cf. Col. 2:8-10; 3:1-6; 3:17). If one is truly believing that God became a man to pay an infinite debt that is rightly owed, and that salvation is simply by grace through faith in Him, victory over the world and its thinking is guaranteed.

V

Section Five

True Christians

Possessors of Eternal Life

Have Fellowship with

the God Who is Truth and Life

God is Truth and Life

1st John 5:6-21: cf. 5:11-13, 20

Chapter 22
Believing God's Testimony

• • • • • •

1 John 5:6-12

6) This is the One who came by water and blood, Jesus Christ; not with the water only, but with the water and with the blood. 7) It is the Spirit who bears witness, because the Spirit is the truth. 8)For there are three that bears witness: the Spirit and the water and the blood; and the three are in agreement. 9) If we receive the witness of men, the witness of God is greater; for the witness of God is this, that He has bore witness concerning His Son.10) The one who believes in the Son of God has the witness in himself; the one who does not believe God has made Him a liar, because he has not believed in the witness that God has given concerning His Son. 11) And the witness is this, that God has given us eternal life, and this life is in His Son. 12) He who has the Son has the life; he who does not have the Son of God does not have the life.

I. **True Christians (Possessors of Eternal Life) Believe God's Testimony Concerning His Son (5:6-12)**

    A.   The Testimony of History and the Holy Spirit (v. 6-9)

         1.   The Testimony of History: Water and Blood (v. 6)

         2.   The Testimony of the Holy Spirit (v. 7-9)

    B.   The Internal Testimony of Eternal Life (v. 10)

    C.   The Content of God's Testimony (v. 11)

    D.   The Verdict (v. 12)

I. True Christians (Possessors of Eternal Life) Believe God's Testimony Concerning His Son (5:6-12)

The thought connection between 5:5 and this section has to do with how faith (5:5), based upon testimony (witness; cf. 5:7ff), brings eternal life. Here there is no direct statement saying, "God is life." It is stated almost as clearly in 5:11-13, 20.

A. The Testimony Through History and the Holy Spirit (v. 6-9)

1. The Testimony of History: Water and Blood (v. 6)

This is the one —

points back to Jesus, the Son of God, in verse 5. Jesus the Son of God is not a myth, but one and the same with the historical man from Nazareth.

came —

the historical reality of Christ's life and ministry (as we now have recorded in the Gospels).

by water —

literally, "through water." This difficult expression most likely refers to Christ's historical baptism, which initiated/inaugurated His public ministry as Savior to redeem mankind. At Christ's baptism God historically testified to the identity of the Person of His Son (cf. Matt. 3:13-17; Mark 1:9-11; Luke 3:21-23). (Another plausible view would understand this as a reference to the historical reality of *Christ's birth* as a man, to redeem men.)

The point remains clear however. John desires to emphasize that the Divine Son of God, who the Father named as Jesus (v. 5), truly became a man to die for men. (The "Christ" didn't just come upon the man Jesus at His baptism and leave Him before His death [the blood], as some of the early Gnostic heretics taught. But Jesus was Divine both before, during and after His baptism—and His death—that through faith in Him, men would have eternal life.)

and blood —

a reference to the Son of God's (v. 5) sacrificial death on the cross to pay the penalty for men's sins (cf. Matt. 27:54; Mark 15:39; Heb. 9:14).

Jesus Christ —

the true Jesus Christ is both God and man. His baptism marks both the start of His public ministry to redeem men and His willing submission to the Spirit of God as the God-Man. His death marked the satisfactory sacrifice for sin.

not with water only, but with the water and the blood —

again most likely a refutation of an ancient heresy called Cerinthian Gnosticism, which said that the "christ spirit" descended on the man Jesus at his baptism and left him before his crucifixion. This would deny the substitutionary atonement that could be accomplished only by a perfect Man (to substitute for imperfect men), who is infinite, eternal God (to make sufficient atonement for offenses against an infinitely holy God).

2. The Testimony of the Holy Spirit (v. 7-9)

And it is the Spirit who bears witness —

This is an ongoing (present tense) testimony. "Witness" speaks of testimony that something is true. It is the Spirit who testifies both internally and externally through the inspired Word of God (John 15:26; 16:13-14; 2 Tim. 3:16-17; 2 Pet. 1:20-21).

because the Spirit is truth —

see especially John 16:13ff (cf. John 17:17).

for there are three that bear witness —

Cf. Duet. 17:6; 19:15; Heb. 10:28-29.

the Spirit and the water and the blood; —

The Spirit uses the apostolic, historical witness to testify of Christ's humanity, deity, and atoning redemption.

and the three are in agreement —

Because the Spirit inspired and employs the Word of God, He is the One who "seals in our hearts the testimony of the water and the blood." (Calvin, as quoted by Stott, p. 180). The Holy Spirit's testimony and the Spirit-inspired testimony of the water and the blood have one purpose—to unequivocally declare that the historical man Jesus of Nazareth is in fact the divine Son of God, only Savior and King. He alone can bring eternal life.

If we receive —

This phrase in the Greek is not a statement of doubt, but a declaration of assumed fact (Burdick, p. 372). In other words, "since we receive the witness of men."

witness of men —

The general truth is that in a court of law, or even in daily life, we accept the testimony of men as true/valid.

the witness of God is greater —

God's witness, represented in v. 6-9 (the Spirit's testimony through the historic baptism and death of Christ—i.e., the Bible) is greater in its "value, dignity, certainty and authority. . . It has greater significance and greater trustworthiness" (Thomas, p. 445). Cf. John 5:30-47 (the witness of John the Baptist, Jesus' works, the Father, and Scripture).

for the witness of God is this —

"This" points to what is to follow. God's witness is seen in verse 10.

that He has born concerning His Son —

God's witness was brought forth in the past, and it has current, abiding results. "His Son" again notes the special relationship and deity of Jesus.

B. The Internal Testimony of Eternal Life (v. 10)

The one who believes in the Son of God —

"believing" (present tense) in, or on, Christ speaks of personal commitment, "surrender to, and implicit trust in His character" (Thomas, p. 449).

has the witness in himself —

The external witness of the Spirit-inspired Word of life becomes the internal testimony of the Spirit *implanted* Word of life. Cf. John 14:15-21, 23.

the one who does not believe God —

this is one who repeatedly will not accept and surrender to what God and His Word say about Jesus.

has made Him a liar —

in this rejecter's mind, God has been and still is a liar about what He has spoken concerning His Son. How can someone call the God who cannot lie (Titus 1:2) a liar? Unbelief— "*because He has not believed the witness that God has borne concerning His Son.*" There is no "in between". It is either belief/trust, or unbelief. Ignorance and noncommittal are tantamount to unbelief.

C. The Content of God's Testimony (v. 11)

God has given us —

Eternal life is a gift given by God (cf. Eph. 2:8-9; Rom. 6:23) to undeserving mankind. "Us" in the context of v. 6-10 speaks of John and his readers (and by application every true believer in Christ Jesus—the Son of God).

eternal life —

Grammatically, the emphasis is on this phrase. It means, *God's kind of life*. Both the quality (here and now) and the duration (future) are eternal.

and this life is in His Son —

This *eternal life* just spoken of is in God's Son. Eternal life is a sovereign gift of God given solely through faith in the Person and work of the Son of God.

The alternative is eternal death and separation from God—hell.

D. The Verdict (v. 12)

has —

a term referring to a personal relationship—wrought by the Holy Spirit, through faith.

All this talk of witnesses and testimony demands a verdict. The verdict is life in Christ, and death for those who reject or simply choose not to decide. "*He who does not have the Son of God does not have the life*" (Cf. John 3:36).

Chapter 23
Having Eternal Life and Answered Prayer

● ● ● ● ● ●

1 John 5:13-17

13) These things I have written to you who believe in the name of the Son of God, so that you may know that you have eternal life. 14) This is the confidence which we have before Him, that, if we ask anything according to His will, He hears us. 15) And if we know that He hears us in whatever we ask, we know that we have the requests which we have asked from Him. 16) If anyone sees his brother committing a sin not leading to death, he shall ask and God will for him give life to those who commit sin not leading to death. There is a sin leading to death; I do not say that he should make request for this. 17) All unrighteousness is sin, and there is a sin not leading to death.

II. True Christians (Possessors of Eternal Life) Have the Certainty of Eternal Life and Answered Prayer (5:13-17)

 A. The Certainty of Eternal Life (v. 13)
   1. The Prerequisite
   2. The Promise
 B. The Certainty of Answered Prayer (v. 14-16)
   1. The Promise (v. 14-15)
   2. The Prerequisite (v. 14)
   3. The Picture/Illustration (v. 16b)
   4. The Point of Limitation (v. 16c)
 C. The Certainty of the Seriousness of Sin (v. 17)

II. True Christians (Possessors of Eternal Life) Have the Certainty of Eternal Life and Answered Prayer (5:13-17)

The Apostle John started this epistle with the testimony of fellowship with God and eternal life (cf. 1:1-3). He is now ending with a very similar emphasis.

A. The Certainty of Eternal Life (v. 13)

These things —

> this term obviously includes verses 11-12, but the reoccurring themes and overall context points to the whole letter as having the purpose of— "that you may know that you have eternal life."

I have written —

> John uses the past tense, which indicates that he is beginning to conclude the epistle. The first-person pronoun signifies that this is John's personal and specific correspondence to his readers (as opposed to the more general apostolic witness concerning the gospel and incarnation of Christ in 1:1-4).

1. The Prerequisite

to you who believe in the name of the Son of God—

> John's purpose in writing was to assure *believers*. This is a present tense/ongoing belief/trust. Belief is not mere mental assent, but an ongoing and growing surrender of your life, trust, hope and well being to Him. "Name" in the Scriptures stands for all that a person is, does, and represents (cf. Ps. 22:22). To believe in the name of the Son of God is to believe that Jesus is the God-Man. Included in this is His deity, humanity, virgin birth, sinless life, substitutionary/sacrificial death and atonement, His resurrection from the grave, and His bodily ascension to the right hand of God the Father. This is to confirm that He is the only Savior and Lord.
>
> The prerequisite to both the assurance of eternal life—and the actual possession of eternal life—is belief in the name of the Son of God.

in order that—

> John's purpose in writing.

2. The Promise

you may know that you have eternal life —

> "This word 'knowing' is used six times in these concluding verses as a means of expressing confidence" (Thomas, p. 456, referencing Brown, p. 608). The promise is the knowledge that you possess eternal life. This knowledge is not acquired through study, but it is a knowledge characterized by certainty and

assurance (intuitively, in a sense). "Have" is a term of possession. John is saying, "I wrote that you may know for sure, automatically in your soul, that you possess God's life—eternal life."

Why is it so important that genuine believers *know* they have eternal life? Such knowledge includes spiritual freedom (cf. John 8:31-36), freedom to serve God (Gal. 5:13), love for God and delightful obedience to Him (Ps. 40:8), freedom to pursue Christ (Col. 3:1-4) and proclaim His excellencies (1 Pet. 2:9-10). Knowing one has eternal life as an irrevocable possession is the key to victory in the Christian life.

B. The Certainty of Answered Prayer (v. 14-16)

1. The Promise (v. 14-15)

confidence which we have —

boldness to approach a loving Father (freedom of speech idea) is the possession of every true believer. Verse 13 indicates freedom of heart and life in God. Verse 14 tells of freedom of access to God.

before Him—

facing/toward God.

if we ask—

this expression speaks of the asking in humility, acknowledging the infinite superiority of God.

anything—

the promise of answered prayer is limited only by the phrase that follows (according to His will).

He hears us—

God listens favorably (Hiebert, p. 256). It is not just that because He is all-knowing He is obligated to hear us. The word carries the idea of listening attentively.

We have the requests which we have asked from Him — The promise continues. It is not just that He hears us, but that He grants the requests. Somehow in the wondrous working of God, "at the moment of prayer, that which is asked for is received" (Burdick, p. 389). The promise is clear—present possession of whatever requests we ask of God. However, as mentioned earlier, there is one prerequisite.

2. The Prerequisite (v. 14)

according to His will (v. 14)—

cf. 1 John 3:22. "In keeping with His plan for us." (Burdick, p. 409). "Thy will be done" (cf. Luke 22:42).

3. The Picture/Illustration (v. 16b)

John moves from the idea of prayer in general, to intercessory prayer in verse 16.

If anyone—

a statement of potentiality.

his brother—

this is another professed believer. (Ultimately only God knows the genuineness of another person's profession).

committing a sin—

literally, "sinning a sin." Remember in 2:1 it says that a believer may commit *acts* of sin, but 1:6-7 and 3:4-10 make it clear that true Christians will not continue in a lifestyle of habitual sin. But here in verse 16 this brother is sinning sin (present tense). There is a certain habitual practice implied in the verb tense. Is John contradicting his earlier statements that Christians don't habitually sin? No—the solution lies in the next phrase contextually, and Romans 7 theologically. All Christians are painfully aware of sinful patterns and habits that plague them. The specific area may differ among Christians, but all have particular areas of weakness where sin seems to habitually manifest itself. Yet, the heart's cry and pursuit of life is one of hatred of sin and a resolution to battle against it.

not leading to death—

"not unto death." This besetting sin is *not a damning lifestyle* of habitual sin that makes one legitimately question this "brother's" genuiness (that is, to wonder if he really is a true Christian).

he shall ask and God will for him give life to those
who commit sin not leading to death—

The promise of answered prayer is illustrated even in intercessory prayer for a brother in Christ who is struggling with besetting sin. God will hear and grant them *fullness of life* (the present experience of the eternal life John has been speaking of) before Him—and grant victory over that sin pattern (in God's timing, not ours).

4. The Point of Limitation (v. 16c)

There is a sin leading to death—

there is no indefinite article in Greek—the phrase reads, "there is sin (a quality of sin) unto death." Answered prayer is not guaranteed when it is concerning a "professing Christian" who is showing no fruit and walking in an unrepentant lifestyle of sin and disregard for God's Word. In other words, the promise of answered prayer does not reach to the unconditional guarantee of the salvation of a "false Christian" who is on the path to spiritual destruction.

I do not say that he should make request for this —

John is not forbidding intercessory prayer on this person's behalf. John does seem to indicate however, that prayer is not the deciding factor in such a case. It is the person's unrepentant heart. John uses a different word here for "request" than he did for "ask" in verse 14. It is possible that the different word might indicate some presumption on the part of the person making the "request."

C. The Certainty of the Seriousness of Sin (v. 17)

All unrighteousness is sin —

Now after making the distinction between a besetting sin in a Christian, and an unregenerate sin pattern in a false professor, John is eager to remind his readers of the seriousness of sin. Anything that does not line up with God's righteous character, as seen in His Word, is sin. It misses the mark and is worthy of death (Rom. 6:23).

and there is [a] sin not leading to death—

"All acts that deviate from God's standard are sins. But of all the acts that are rightly classified as sins, there are some that do not lead to death, and it is for these that prayer may be made with full confidence" (Burdick, p. 392).

Not all sin classifies one as a false professor of the faith (cf. Rom. 7).

Chapter 24
Having New Relationships

• • • • • •

1 John 5:18-20

18) We know that no one who is born of God sins; but He who was born of God keeps him, and the evil one does not touch him. 19) We know that we are of God, and that the whole world lies in the power of the evil one. 20) And we know that the Son of God has come, and has given us understanding in order that we might know Him who is true; and we are in Him who is true, in His Son Jesus Christ. This is the true God and eternal life.

> III. **True Christians (Possessors of Eternal Life) Know the Truth about Their Relationship to Sin, the World, and God Himself (5:18-20)**
>
> A. We Are No Longer Friends of Sin (v. 18)
> B. We Are No Longer Citizens of This World (v. 19)
> C. We Are No Longer Estranged from God (v. 20)

III. True Christians (Possessors of Eternal Life) Know the Truth About Their Relationship to Sin, the World, and God Himself (5:18-20)

A. We Are No Longer Friends of Sin (v. 18)

We know—

this is the absolute, assured type of knowledge that is known intuitively.

no one who is born of God sins—

literally rendered, "everyone who is born of God is not sinning." There are absolutely, unequivocally no exceptions, as indicated by "no one." Because a genuine Christian is currently standing in the state of having been born of God, he does not live in a condition characterized by "sinning." Again, it is obvious that John is not talking about sinless perfection (cf. 1:7-2:1). He however is talking about the incompatibility of being born again and practicing sin. Sin has been deposed from being a voting citizen to being a foreigner in the life of a believer.

but He who was born of God keeps him—

John changes the tense of the verb "begotten/born" to indicate a definite reference to Jesus Christ. "Keeps" speaks of continual protection. Jesus Christ—the only begotten God (the eternal 2nd Person of the Trinity)—continually protects those who have been born of God (true believers). A genuine Christian's relationship with sin is portrayed as antagonistic, not as friendly. We as believers can't take credit for victory over habitual/lifestyle sin (though we are definitely called by God to fight sin, mourn over sin, and pray against sin). In the final analysis, however, Christ is the One who keeps us (cf. Phil. 2:12-13).

and the evil one does not touch him—

The Greek word translated "touch" here conveys a much richer meaning than our English word can communicate. It means "to fasten oneself to, cling to, lay hold of" (Abbott-Smith, p. 56). The devil (the evil one) cannot lay hold of us, or fasten himself to us/cling to us. This is a present, abiding reality.

True Christians may meet sin occasionally (or possibly at frequent intervals), but there is no longer an abiding love-relationship to sin.

B. We Are No Longer Citizens of This World (v. 19)

we are of God—

speaks of origin. God is the genuine Christian's source of life and is his dwelling place. Christians are born of God (5:1).

and the whole world lies in the power of the evil one —

The world system, as a whole, lies fast asleep in the lap of Satan. There is no struggle or fight against him. The picture is one of contentment in the arms of the evil one. The truth about the world is that it is content to be under the control and influence of the devil.

Though believers have national identities and hold various citizenships, we are aliens and strangers in this world (cf. Heb. 11:9-11; 1 Pet. 1:1) — Ambassadors for Christ to a lost and dying world yes (2 Cor. 5:20), but citizens, no!

C. We Are No Longer Estranged from God (v. 20)

given us understanding—

> "the capacity to understand" (Burdick, p. 394), with the result that we might know.

that we might know—

> "know" here is a different word than previously used in "we know" (v. 18, 19, 20). Here the word indicates a growing in knowledge.

Him who is true—

> literally, "the True One." The word means genuine/real as opposed to false/counterfeit/imaginary (The real God. The God who is really God—not a made up, created idol of men's wisdom and imagination).

and we are in Him who is true—

> again relational language (cf. 2:24; 3:24; 4:4, 12-13, 15-16). True Christians have an intimate, personal relationship with the only One who is truly God. We are in Him—the Creator—the One who spoke, and out of nothing came all creation—the King of kings and Lord of lords.

in His Son Jesus Christ—

> again relational language, this time applied to the Son (cf. 2:22-23).

This is the true God and eternal life—

> The One who is perfectly revealed only in Jesus Christ is the true God and eternal life. To have a relationship with Jesus Christ is to be in a relationship with the true God and have eternal life (cf. John 14:1-9; John 11:25). Genuine Christianity is worshipping the true God, in and through Jesus Christ His Son—Who is the true God and eternal life. This sentence may well be the climax of the entire epistle.

Chapter 25
Guarding from Idols

● ● ● ● ● ●

1 John 5:21

Little children, guard yourselves from idols.

IV. True Christians (Possessors of Eternal Life) Must Guard Themselves from Idols (5:21)

    A. What is an Idol?

    B. How Can We Guard Ourselves from Idols?

D. True Christians (Possessors of Eternal Life) Must Guard Themselves from Idols (5:21)

Verse 18 spoke of God's sovereign protection. In verse 21 the grammatical emphasis is on the Christian's responsibility.

Little Children —

John's final exhortation again is prefaced by this term of love and affection.

1. What is an Idol?

The context of v. 20 indicates any false view of Jesus Christ/God. This would include any philosophy or religion that would seek to diminish the supreme majesty and glory of Jesus Christ as Lord or deny the sufficiency of His atonement, death and resurrection.

Guard yourselves —

"Let go and let God" is not the mandate of God's Word (Phil. 2:12-13; 2 Pet. 1:3-11). We are to keep ourselves from idols. A command and plea to be watchful and vigilant against the idols.

2. How Can I Guard Myself from Idols?

See Colossians 2:8-10; 3:1-4; 1 John 4:1-6.

Bibliography

Abbott-Smith, G. *A Manual Greek Lexicon of the New Testament*. T & T Clark. 1994.

Barker, Glenn W. "1 John" in *Expositor's Bible Commentary*. Zondervan. 1981.

Brown, Colin. *The New International Dictionary of New Testament Theology*. Zondervan. 1998.

Burdick, Donald W. *The Letters of John The Apostle*. Moody Press. 1985.

Gooding, A. M. S. "1, 2, & 3 John" in *Ritchie New Testament Commentaries*. John Ritchie Ltd. 1987.

Hiebert, D. Edmond. *The Epistles of John*. Bob Jones University Press. 1991.

MacArthur, John F. *The Glory of Heaven*. Crossway Books. 1996.

MacArthur, John F. *The Love of God*. Word Publishing. 1996.

Meeter, John E. *Benjamin B. Warfield, Selected Shorter Writings*, Vol. 1. Presbyterian and Reformed Publishing Company. 1970.

Morris, Leon. *The Apostolic Preaching of the Cross*. Eerdmans. 1994.

Stott, John R. W. *The Epistles of John*. Eerdmans. 1981.

Thomas, Robert L. *Exegetical Digest of 1 John*. Published by author. 1984.

Vine, Unger, and White. *Vines Complete Expository Dictionary of Old and New Testament Words*. Thomas Nelson Publishers. 1985.

Wallace, Daniel B. *Greek Grammar Beyond the Basics*. Zondervan. 1996.

Wiersbe, Warren W. *Be Real*. Victor Books. 1972.

●●●●●●

Study Guide

This study guide and the questions contained within are based upon the NASB version of the Bible.

The study guide may be freely copied for in class use only, but may not be reproduced for profit.

Study Guide

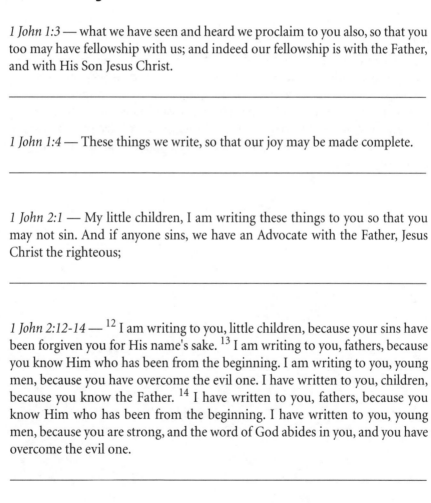

Study Guide Introduction
● ● ● ● ● ●

From each of the following references summarize in one word or phrase, the author's reasons for writing 1 John.

1 John 1:3 — what we have seen and heard we proclaim to you also, so that you too may have fellowship with us; and indeed our fellowship is with the Father, and with His Son Jesus Christ.

_____

1 John 1:4 — These things we write, so that our joy may be made complete.

_____

1 John 2:1 — My little children, I am writing these things to you so that you may not sin. And if anyone sins, we have an Advocate with the Father, Jesus Christ the righteous;

_____

1 John 2:12-14 — [12] I am writing to you, little children, because your sins have been forgiven you for His name's sake. [13] I am writing to you, fathers, because you know Him who has been from the beginning. I am writing to you, young men, because you have overcome the evil one. I have written to you, children, because you know the Father. [14] I have written to you, fathers, because you know Him who has been from the beginning. I have written to you, young men, because you are strong, and the word of God abides in you, and you have overcome the evil one.

_____

_____

1 John 2:26 — These things I have written to you concerning those who are trying to deceive you.

_____

_____

1 John 5:13 — These things I have written to you who believe in the name of the Son of God, so that you may know that you have eternal life.

_____

_____

Note Well

The overall context of 1 John indicates that 5:13 is the over-arching theme and purpose of the epistle. It is important as you study this epistle that you keep asking yourself, "what does this section have to do with the reasons the apostle John wrote the book, especially the reason stated in 1 John 5:13?" It is vital to the proper understanding of this epistle to realize that the author is giving us pictures of one who already has eternal life, *not prerequisites for gaining eternal life.*

I John Chapter 1

● ● ● ● ● ●

Read 1 John 1:1-4

What does 1 John 1:1-4 have to do with eternal life and knowing you have eternal life?

_____

_____

Who is Eternal Life according to 1 John 1:1-4?

_____

_____

What is the definition of fellowship? (cf. 2 Peter 1:4; Luke 5:10)

_____

_____

According to 1 John 1:3, who is it that Christians have fellowship with?

_____

Read 1 John 1:5-7

In 1 John 1:5 Christians have fellowship with the God who is _____.
(In other words, how is God's Person/character defined?)

In 1 John 1:5-7, true Christians (possessors of eternal life) are characterized by

_____.

Biblically define "light" (see 2 Cor. 4:6; John 3:19-21; Eph. 5:8-14).

_____

_____

What does "walking in the light" look like in your personal life?

_____

_____

_____

_____

_____

_____

Read 1 John 1:8-10

In 1 John 1:8-10, true Christians (possessors of eternal life) are characterized by _____.

What does it mean to "confess" our sins? (cf. Ps. 51:1-12; Ps. 5:4-5; Acts 19:18-19).

_____

_____

_____

_____

Would you say you are a person who owns up to, and turns away from his sin before God and others?

_____

_____

_____

I John Chapter 2

Read 1 John 2:1-2

In 1 John 2:1-2 give at least two reasons why true Christians (possessors of eternal life) can be encouraged

_____

_____

Do these assurances give you the freedom to continue to sin?

_____

_____

Why or why not?

_____

_____

_____

Read 1 John 2:3-6

In 1 John 2:3-6, true Christians (possessors of eternal life) are characterized by

_____.

According to 1 John 2:3-6 what is another word for commands?

_____

Do you seek for God regularly in His Word (the Bible)?

_____

_____

Read 1 John 2:7-11

In 1 John 2:7-11, true Christians (possessors of eternal life) are characterized

by _____.

Define "love" biblically (cf. John 3:16; John 15:13).

_____

_____

Do you love other believers?

_____

How is that evidenced in your life?

_____

_____

_____

_____

Read 1 John 2:12-14

In 1 John 2:12-14, true Christians (possessors of eternal life) can be encouraged
because they _____. (see especially verse 12)

What is the basis for that?

_____

_____

_____

_____

Read 1 John 2:15-17

In 1 John 2:15-17, true Christians (possessors of eternal life) do not
_____.

Give three reasons why?

_____

_____

_____

In what ways do you flirt with the world?

_____

_____

_____

_____

Read 1 John 2:18-28

In 1 John 2:18-28, true Christians (possessors of eternal life) know the
_____ (see especially verses 20-21).

Why? (see verses 20-21, 27)

_____

_____

_____

Give at least two results of the previous two answers (cf. verses 19, 23).

_____

_____

_____

_____

Read 1 John 2:29

True Christians have fellowship with the God who is _____.

(In other words, how is God's Person/character defined?)

Therefore true Christians (possessors of eternal life) are characterized by

_____.

I John Chapter 3

• • • • • •

Read 1 John 3:1-3

In 1 John 3:1-3, true Christians (possessors of eternal life) can be encouraged because they have the promise of _____.

What is the basis for their hope?

_____

_____

_____

_____

When will their hope be fully realized?

_____

_____

_____

_____

What is the present result of their hope?

_____

_____

_____

_____

Read 1 John 3:4-10a

In 1 John 3:4-10a, true Christians (possessors of eternal life) are characterized

by _____.

What is your attitude toward sin that you see in your life?

_____

_____

_____

Do you think the Apostle John is saying that a true Christian never sins (cf. 1 John 1:8-10)?

_____

_____

_____

Read 1 John 3:10b-24

In 1 John 3:10b-24, true Christians (possessors of eternal life) are characterized

by _____.

Do you see practical expressions of love as characteristic of your life?

_____

_____

_____

What truth gives even greater assurance to us than merely seeing external deeds of love (cf. verse 20b)?

_____

_____

_____

I John Chapter 4

• • • • • •

Read 1 John 4:1-6

In 1 John 4:1-6, true Christians (possessors of eternal life) must _____.

What is the first test of truth? (v. 2-3)

_____

_____

_____

What is the second test of truth? (v. 5-6).

_____

_____

_____

_____

Read 1 John 4:7-12

True Christians have fellowship with the God who is _____.

(In other words, how is God's Person/character described?)

In 1 John 4:7-12, true Christians (possessors of eternal life) are characterized

by _____.

Give at least two reasons why.

_____

_____

_____

_____

_____

Read 1 John 4:13-19

In 1 John 4:13-19, true Christians (possessors of eternal life) can be encouraged

because they _____.

What is the basis of their assurance (give at least two answers)?

(see especially verses 14 and 19).

1) _____

2) _____

3) _____

Read 1 John 4:20-5:5

In 1 John 4:20-5:5, true Christians (possessors of eternal life) cannot separate

what three aspects of their lives?

1) _____

2) _____

3) _____

Therefore: They _____ the _____

(see especially verses 4-5).

I John Chapter 5

• • • • • •

Read 1 John 5:6-12

True Christians have fellowship with the God who is _____ (v. 6; cf. John 4:24) and _____ (implied from verses 11-12).

Therefore: True Christians (possessors of eternal life) believe _____ and have _____.

Read 1 John 5:13-17

In 1 John 5:13 what is the only prerequisite for having eternal life?

1 John 5:13-17, true Christians can be encouraged that they have the certainty of _____ and _____.

What are some effects these two certainties should make in our lives?

_____

_____

_____

_____

_____

Read 1 John 5:18-20

In 1 John 5:18-20, true Christians (possessors of eternal life) know the truth

about their relationship to _____, _____ and

_____.

Assess your relationship with these three entities.

_____

_____

_____

_____

Read 1 John 5:21

In 1 John 5:21, possessors of eternal life are to _____.

What is an "idol"?

_____

_____

Summarize three main proofs that the Apostle John gives his readers so that they may know they have eternal life (what have been the reoccurring characteristics of possessors of eternal life? Hint: see 1 John 4:20-5:5).

_____

_____

_____

Do you think these characteristics of believers must be seen in perfection to have the assurance of eternal life? Give proof from 1 John for your answer (see 1:7-2:2).

_____

_____

_____

_____

Are the sections in 1 John requirements for salvation, or evidences of salvation that bring assurance?

_____

_____

_____

_____

_____

In 1 John 5:13, what do you think it means to believe in the "Name" of the Son of God?

_____

_____

_____

_____

_____

Do you see the evidences of eternal life in your own daily living?

_____

_____

_____

_____

_____